W9-BEO-747

The Episcopal Handbook

The Episcopal Handbook

REVISED EDITION

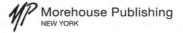 Morehouse Publishing
NEW YORK

THE EPISCOPAL HANDBOOK

Copyright © 2015 Church Publishing Incorporated. All rights reserved. Except for brief quotations in critical articles or reviews, no part of this book may be reproduced in any manner without prior written permission from the publisher. Write to: Permissions, Church Publishing Inc., 19 East 34th Street, New York, NY 10016.

Part of this book was originally published as the Lutheran Handbook © 2005, Augsburg Fortress.

Elements of Worst-Case Scenario Survival Handbook® trade dress have been used with permission of and under license from Quirk Productions, Inc. Based on the trade dress of The Worst-Case Scenario Survival Handbook Series, by Joshua Piven and David Borgenicht, published by Chronicle Books, LLC. Worst-Case Scenario® and The Worst-Case Scenario Survival Handbook Series® are registered trademarks of Quirk Productions, Inc., 215 Church Street, Philadelphia, PA 19106.

Scripture quotations are from the New Revised Standard Version Bible, copyright © 1989, Division of Christian Education of the National Council of the Churches of Christ in the United States of America. Used by permission. All rights reserved.

Pages 202–20: Glossary adapted from *Altar Guild and Sacristy Handbook,* by S. Anita Stauffer, copyright © 2000 Augsburg Fortress; also adapted from *Words of Our Worship: A Practical Liturgical Dictionary* by Charles Mortimer Guilbert, copyright © 1988 Church Hymnal Corporation; and from The Book of Common Prayer.

Map image on pages 96–97 by Jennifer Prather
New brand development editor: Kristofer Skrade
2014 Revision Editor: Tobias Stanislas Haller BSG
Editors: Barbara S. Wilson and Arlene Flancher; Susan Erdey
Production editor: Ryan Masteller
Interior illustrator: Brenda Brown, Dorothy Thompson Perez
Interior layout: Rose Design

Contributing writers: Rod Anderson, Chip Borgstadt, Ramona S. Bouzard, Walter C. Bouzard, Eric Burtness, Louis R. Carlozo, Carol Carver, Chris Duckworth, Susan T. Erdey, Rod Hank, Paul N. Hanson, Susan Houglum, Mark J. Jackson, Rolf A. Jacobson, Mark D. Johns, Mark K. Johnson, Ken Sundet Jones, James Kasperson, Timothy Keyl, Charles R. Lane, Susan M. Lang, Catherine Malotky, Mark C. Mattes, Sally Messner, Jennifer Moland-Kovash, Seth Moland-Kovash, Jan Nunley, Paul Owens, Rebecca Ninke, Marc Ostlie-Olson, Frank L.

Tedeschi, Tom Teichmann, Megan J. Thorvilson, Megan Torgerson, Erik Ullestad, Darin Wiebe, Hans Wiersma, Chris Yaw, and Steven Zittergruen

Library of Congress Cataloging-in-Publication Data

A catalog record of this book is available from the Library of Congress.

ISBN-13: 978-0-8192-2956-4 (pbk.)

ISBN-13: 978-0-8192-2957-1 (ebook)

The paper used in this publication meets the minimum requirements of American National Standard for Information Sciences–Permanence of Paper for Printed Library Materials, ANSI Z329.48-1984.

Manufactured in Canada

CONTENTS

Everyday Stuff 99

Bible Stuff   137

BRIEF EXPLANATION OF THE EPISCOPAL CHURCH SHIELD

The Episcopal Church shield is a familiar symbol found on signs, in print ads, and on many a website. It is usually accompanied by the words, "The Episcopal Church Welcomes You," often with information about a local church's location and worship schedule.

The shield and the corresponding flag were officially adopted by General Convention in 1940; both are rich in symbolism. The shield is usually presented in red, white, and blue (see cover). The red cross on a white field is an ancient Christian symbol, white representing the purity of Jesus and red representing his sacrifice on the cross and the blood of Christian martyrs. The red cross is known as the cross of St. George, patron saint of England, and indicates the Episcopal Church's descent from the Church of England. The blue field in the upper left is the color traditionally associated with the Blessed Virgin Mary and is symbolic of Jesus' human nature, which he received from his mother. The X-shaped cross is the cross of St. Andrew, patron saint of Scotland, and recalls the Episcopal Church's indebtedness to Scottish bishops for the consecration of the first American bishop, Samuel Seabury, in 1784. The St. Andrew's cross is made up of nine smaller cross-crosslets that stand for the representatives of the Church in the nine states who met in Philadelphia in 1789 to adopt the constitution of the Episcopal Church.

These representatives came from Connecticut, Maryland, Massachusetts, Pennsylvania, New Jersey, New York, South Carolina, Virginia, and Delaware.

INTRODUCTION

Just before the turn of the millennium, a small, yellow paperback appeared on the shelves and check-out counters of bookstores and hip, urban retailers. *The Worst Case Scenario Survival Handbook* showed the world how to live through earthquakes, fend off sharks, and stay alive in quicksand. Its frank demeanor, adventuresome spirit, and naked sincerity struck a chord with a nervous Y2K populace preoccupied with preparation. The book was a huge hit, spawning numerous spin-offs (eventually including *The Worst Case Scenario Survival Handbook: Weddings*), a TV show, and even a board game. There seemed to be no end to our curious appetite for instruction and guidance no matter how remote the possibility of real-life application.

We all like to be prepared.

This includes those of us who participate in more mundane (and hopefully safer) activities like attending Sunday worship at an Episcopal church. The particularities of receiving communion or the intricacies of congregations singing four-part harmony can be mystifying to the newcomer. Liturgical churches can be intimidating when we don't know what's going on. We need "survival" lessons of our own. Granted, the parallel between enduring a bad sermon and surviving quicksand is certainly a stretch, as one could actually enjoy floating in quicksand—for a time.

So in the spirit—if not in the letter—of survival handbooks, we have endeavored to outline, with minimal blather and nominal peril, the great joys and wonders of life in the Episcopal Church. These days we're an increasingly diverse collection of Christians from varied backgrounds (70 percent come to us from other traditions) who gather around shared convictions about prayer, liturgy, church government, and—most importantly—the life and ministry of Jesus Christ. We're a place that welcomes random questions and eccentric personalities. We're a peculiar people whose spiritual arc bends more toward boundless hope and a reasonable faith than hardened surety and entrenched absolutism. Convictions are solid, but questions are welcomed.

Episcopalians find comfort, nurture, fellowship, and encouragement in our faith communities. And we believe the Almighty is not finished with us yet. We believe—now more than ever—that we provide a uniquely fulfilling and vital role in the panoply of modern Christian experiences.

The pages that follow are abbreviated invitations to much longer conversations that can be continued with further reading online or in books or other resources, or by visiting one of the thousands of neighborhood Episcopal congregations. We have chosen to write some of what follows in a light-hearted manner, because it comes naturally to us. Episcopalians laugh a lot, though we can be serious and solemn as the occasion requires. This is a healthy response to a colorful heritage—and perhaps the sign of God's continued hand upon such a flawed and faulty vessel. How else does one respond to such a checkered past?

Our goal is to extend to Episcopalians and non-Episcopalians alike a generous invitation to learn more about our particular expression of the Christian faith. Our way of living out the Gospel of Jesus Christ may not suit everyone, but it does suit us, and it may suit you, especially if you've read this far.

So relax and prepare for possibility over peril, imagination over anxiety, and dreams over danger. We're here to be your guide.

A Note on the 2014 Revision

As Isaac Watt's hymn puts it, "Time, like an ever-rolling stream, bears all our years away" (*The Hymnal 1982*, Hymn 680). The same can be said of survival manuals and guidebooks, such as the one in your hand at the moment. While some things are the same yesterday and today, few things remain the same forever. Given the need to reprint in 2014, the publishers felt it was a good time to issue an update. This also provided an opportunity to incorporate feedback from the earlier edition, and to make a number of changes. These include:

- correcting a few errors—in the hope of not introducing new ones, for which your continued correction is urged;
- updating factual information;
- focusing more directly on specifically Episcopalian personalities in the biography and arts section, which in the earlier version included more non-Episcopalian Anglicans—not to diminish the importance of our Anglican heritage, but in order to highlight the contributions Episcopalians have made *to* that heritage;
- adjusting some of the less successful attempts at humor, while still keeping a light touch; and
- adding additional sections addressing topics that were not covered, but were suggested by readers.

Please don't hesitate to provide additional feedback, with an eye to the next edition; and thank you for reading.

Tobias Stanislas Haller BSG
2014 Revision Editor

CHURCH STUFF

HOW TO SURVIVE A BAPTISM

We start with baptism because this is the sacrament of beginnings.

Episcopalians understand baptism as full initiation into Christ's body, the Church, which is why we often start early—with infants.

Most baptisms are performed in a church setting where priests or bishops preside. But in an emergency, any baptized person can baptize.

The essence of the ceremony boils down to water and words: one sentence, "N., I baptize you in the Name of the Father, and of the Son, and of the Holy Spirit," said by the officiant as water is poured over the candidate's head, or as they are immersed.

Other than in emergency baptism, it is normal for there to be a time of preparation for candidates—or the sponsors (including godparents) in the case of a young child or infant. The role of sponsors or godparents is to support those being baptized and to make promises on behalf of children. The whole congregation also joins in by pledging their support for those being baptized, whether children or adults.

Often a baptismal candle is lit and presented to show the newly baptized person has received the light of Christ. It's appropriate to light these candles annually, on one's baptismal anniversary.

After baptism in water, the priest or bishop traces the cross on the baptized person's forehead, often with anointing oil (called "chrism"), and declares that he or she is sealed by the Holy Spirit and marked as Christ's own forever.

The container that holds the water is typically called a font. Many fonts have eight sides as a reminder of the "eighth day"—the day of circumcision for the Hebrews and a day of beginnings—the first day after seven.

Baptism is received as a sign of trust in Christ and joining in his death and life. In the case of infant baptism, the child relies upon the care and faith of his or her parents and sponsors—and the whole congregation—as they grow in maturity and knowledge of God.

Water is an ancient symbol of cleansing and deliverance, evoking both the Creation and the deliverance at the Red Sea. The Lord uses it to wash away sins and make us new. It is the tangible and effective symbol of the invisible power of God's forgiveness and acceptance, and of the grace of new life in God.

Note: Episcopalians baptize people of all ages—not just infants. And we recognize all baptisms performed in other churches that use water and the threefold invocation of God in the rite.

HOW TO RECEIVE COMMUNION

The Sacrament of the Holy Eucharist (also called the Holy Communion, the Divine Liturgy, the Lord's Supper, or the Mass) is the central event in Episcopal worship. All five senses are engaged, and it is the most interactive part of worship. Local customs for receiving communion can be confusing or complex, so it's wise to pay attention and prepare.

Determine which method of distribution is used. Verbal directions or printed instructions will likely be given prior to the distribution of communion. The most common methods for communion of the Wine are the common cup and intinction.

Note: Many congregations commune gathered at the altar rail as the ministers move from person to person; some practice "continuous communion" with the Bread and the Wine administered by ministers standing at a specific location (a "station"), and some do both. Standing and kneeling to receive are both common.

Look for guidance from the usher. The usher will direct the people in each row or pew to stand and take a place in line to approach the altar or station.

Proceed to the place at which communion is administered, at the rail or a station. Best practice is often simply to follow the person in front of you and do as they do. (Hint: Don't sit right on the aisle on your first visit; that may give you a pew-mate to follow.)

Kneel if that is the custom and you are able. Congregations that commune at altar rails normally provide comfortable kneelers. When this happens, remember to stand slowly to avoid jostling your neighbor. Assist people who are elderly with altar rail navigation when they need help.

Common Cup

Receive the Bread. Extend your hands with palms facing up, resting one hand on the other. The minister will place the bread in your open hands, while saying something during the administration, either, "The Body of Christ, the Bread of Heaven," or some other form of words. You may respond, "Amen," and then either raise your palm to your mouth or take the Bread with the other hand and eat It.

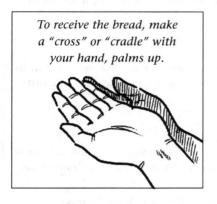

To receive the bread, make a "cross" or "cradle" with your hand, palms up.

Note: Bread may be distributed as fragments of a loaf or a large wafer, or in smaller, individual wafer form.

Receive the Wine. The Wine will be administered in a large cup or chalice, as a sign of unity. The server will present the chalice with a form of words. "Amen" is again appropriate. Assist the server by placing one hand alongside the cup and the other guiding its base. Help the server guide the chalice to your lips, but don't try to take it. Drink a small sip from the chalice.

Intinction

Note: The word *intinction* is from the Latin word *intingere,* which means "to dip."

Receive the Bread. Follow the same procedure as above, but *do not eat the Bread yet.*

Receive the Wine. The preferred method is for the server administering the chalice (the "chalicist") to take the Bread from your palm, dip it in the Wine, and then place it on your tongue. This is preferred because the chalicist can see the level of the Wine and dip appropriately. If the local custom is for the individual to intinct, take the Bread between two fingers and wait for the chalicist to hold the chalice low enough for you to see into it. Dip just the edge of the Bread into the wine, raise your hand carefully to avoid touching the rim of the chalice, then place the Bread in your mouth.

One Kind

Some people do not wish, or are unable, to receive Communion in both forms (Bread and Wine). Receiving only one element counts as full participation in communion.

Once You Have Communed

Return to your seat. If communion is distributed in one continuous line, you may immediately return to your seat. The same may be the case at an altar rail, but . . .

Wait until your "rail" is complete. If you're being served as a group at the altar rail, it may be local custom to wait until all other worshipers in that "set" have received before returning to your seat. This is an appropriate time to close your eyes, pray, or listen to the communion music.

Continue to participate when seated. After returning to your place, you may join the congregation in singing communion hymns, or pray in silence. A particularly suitable prayer is on page 834 of the Prayer Book.

Be Aware

- Some congregations offer the option of non-alcoholic Wine in addition to Wine during communion, or gluten-free Bread for those with allergies. Verbal or written instructions will be given prior to distribution so you will be able to identify these options.

- After receiving the Bread and Wine, there is no need to say "Thank you" to the server. The Eucharist itself is "the Great Thanksgiving" to God, whose gifts are the Body and Blood. If you wish, "Amen" is appropriate.
- Pastoral blessings are often available for any who are not communing. Simply cross your arms over your chest if you wish to receive such a blessing.

WHY YOU WON'T GET SICK SHARING A COMMUNION CUP

In this age of readily available hand sanitizer, it may appear a bit unseemly for a whole church full of people to drink out of the same chalice. Won't I catch a cold or pass on the flu? Actually, sharing a common cup isn't as hazardous as one might suspect. And the hand sanitizer is a clue as to why: hands are a preferred path for spreading germs.

Most Episcopal churches use real wine—and then some; most use fortified wine such as port or sherry. This has a higher alcohol content, killing off many germs.

Not long ago a Canadian doctor named David Gould did research into illnesses passed through a common cup and found church-goers more likely to get sick from airborne infections than from a shared chalice. "If communion cups were a danger, there would be cases of mass infections," he wrote; and there aren't. Moreover, the ministers, who regularly consume anything remaining in the chalice, generally have very good health and longevity.

However, if you still feel uncomfortable drinking the Wine (or are a recovering alcoholic), this is not essential to receiving Communion. Episcopalians believe Christ is equally present in both the consecrated Bread and the Wine, so receiving one assures you of full participation and Christ's presence through the Sacrament.

HOW TO SING A HYMN (AND WHY YOU MIGHT WANT TO)

Music is an important part of the Episcopal tradition and an enjoyable way to build community. (See page 91 for "Ten Famous Hymns Written by Episcopalians.") One can sing hymns without demonstrable emotion, but many otherwise prim and proper Episcopalians appropriately channel emotion into their hymn singing and are therefore loud.

Locate hymns in advance. As you prepare for worship, consult the worship bulletin or the hymn board to find numbers for the day's hymns. Bookmark these pages in the hymnal using an offering envelope or bulletin insert. Many choir members have long since learned the virtue of Post-it Notes (invented by a choir member to keep his place in his hymnal!).

Familiarize yourself with the hymns. Note the lyricist and composer credits, the years they lived, and the tune name. Note how the hymn is categorized in the hymnal. *The Hymnal 1982* groups hymns into categories, such as "Holy Eucharist" and "Christmas."

Don't be afraid to ask for help. Using a hymnal can be confusing. If your neighbor seems to be in the right place, ask them to help you find the correct page; this may be a good way to meet a member of the congregation.

Adopt a posture suited to good vocal performance. Hold the hymnal up rather than arching over to see it. Place one hand under the spine of the binding, leaving the other hand free to hold the pages. Keep your chin up so your voice projects outward.

Begin singing. If the hymn is unfamiliar, listen to others for the first verse, then join in the melody for the second. If you read music, explore the harmony parts during the remaining verses. Loud-singing neighbors may or may not be in tune, so follow them with caution. (Hymns meant to be sung in unison will usually only have the melody.)

Focus on the hymn's verbal content. Some of the lyrics may connect with a Scripture reading of the day. Certain ones may be especially inspiring.

Avoid dreariness. Enjoy the music. Sing with energy and feeling.

Be Aware

- Hymnals are not just for use at church. Consider ordering a personal copy of *The Hymnal 1982* for further reference and study. Hymnals also make excellent baptism or confirmation gifts.

- Some hymns use words and phrases that are difficult to understand (such as, "Here I raise my Ebenezer," from the hymn "Come Thou Fount of Every Blessing" in *Lift Every Voice and Sing II*). Use a dictionary or a Bible with a concordance to clear up any uncertainty.

- Some church organists and music directors like to improvise between verses or to play alternate harmonies on some of the verses. This is part of their ministry in adding richness to the worship, so listen carefully as well as singing joyfully. This is especially important if you are singing the harmony parts while the organist is playing an alternate harmonization. Composer Charles Ives was a church organist, and perhaps this was how he developed some of his distinctive style.

HOW TO RESPOND WHEN SOMEONE SITS IN YOUR PEW . . .

. . . or you sit in theirs! We all carry a bubble of personal space. For some people, it's several feet. For others, it's about a millimeter. Wherever on the spectrum you happen to fall, there are certain situations in which we invite visitors into our little sphere of experience—such as at church. Furthermore, human beings are territorial in nature and sometimes see strangers inside the bubble as an affront. These situations need not be cause for alarm.

Smile and greet those who are new to you. Often they may be visitors to the congregation—and you may be the first face they see. Make courteous eye contact so they know you mean it, shake hands with them, with no impression that anyone has done something wrong. (The days of "pew rental"—in which the church was funded by the actual rented ownership of pews—is long past, though many have their "favorite spot.")

Make this "intrusion" an opportunity. Remember, no one owns the pew; all just borrow it once a week. If you discover someone in your favorite place, take the opportunity to get out of your rut and sit someplace new. This will physically emphasize a change in your perspective and may yield new spiritual discoveries.

If you can tell that your new friends feel uncomfortable, despite your efforts to the contrary, make an extra effort at courtesy. Consider the possibility of an after-church brunch.

WHAT ARE ALL THOSE BOOKS IN THE PEW?

Episcopalians are a people of the book. Actually, several books.

While the Bible is the foundation of our library, it is not the only book we rely on to help us worship. That's why you'll find several books in the pews of most Episcopal churches.

The most common (by far) is the 1979 edition of the Book of Common Prayer (BCP). Inside you'll find over 1,000 pages of some of the richest and most beautiful liturgies ever written. In addition to regular Sunday morning worship, the Prayer Book provides liturgies for Baptism, Matrimony, and Burial (sometimes humorously described as the "rites of the three elements"—water, rice, and earth). There are also many prayers, historical documents, and much more. It abounds in scriptural imagery and phraseology. We like to think of the Book of Common Prayer as the Bible rearranged for worship.

A second book is *The Hymnal 1982*. This includes a rich collection of service music (in the front section) and hymns. Some of these selections are over a thousand years old. Others are just a few decades new. One thing they all have in common is that they're widely considered to be some of the best worship music ever written—not just in the last forty years, but in the last twenty centuries.

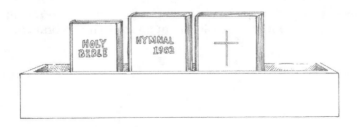

Other books you may find in the pews include Bibles or Lectionaries (a volume containing the Scripture passages read in worship) and additional hymnals such as *Lift Every Voice and Sing II, Wonder, Love and Praise, Voices Found*, and *My Heart Sings Out*. We told you Episcopalians like to sing! You may also find visitors' brochures and the occasional coloring book (proof that not every Episcopalian knows how to read).

While some people consider written prayers and prescribed liturgy tedious and lacking spontaneity, it can also be said that writing things down is a high form of respect and sincerity. The care with which these books are written, edited, and arranged bespeaks the reverence, foresight, and values Episcopalians bring to their worship—even if this also means they have to bring their glasses.

About Bulletins

In earlier days, before photocopying became available, most parishes would indicate which hymns were to be sung by putting up numbers on one or more "hymn boards"—wooden racks designed for that purpose. Many churches still have hymn boards and put the hymn numbers on display even though they also produce a printed bulletin. These bulletins can vary from a simple sheet listing the order of service with page and hymn numbers, to a fully printed order of service with everything to be said or sung, including the music. Most churches do something in between these two extremes. Often churches will provide additional sheets with parish news or prayer intentions or announcements. Not only do these provide important information, but they can serve as handy bookmarks for you to place in the hymnal.

Some churches have gone high-tech and use projectors to display the lyrics or music, or other worship texts. Welcome to the twenty-first century.

WHY IS EVERYBODY KNEELING?

Subjects do it before kings, some do it when proposing marriage, and many Christians do it when they go to church:

kneeling.

It's an act of respect for authority, honor to royalty, and contrition for sin. It is one of three basic positions many Episcopalians assume in the course of regular Sunday worship.

Typically, we kneel to confess our sins, to receive absolution, and to pray (although standing for prayer is the more ancient posture). In recent years there has been in some places a trend away from kneeling as often or as long. It's not because we've gotten lazy, but in order to recover an ancient sensibility toward worship: the idea that Christian worship is not only about penitence but about rejoicing in the forgiveness Jesus brings.

So when we stand we do so to show respect, for example, during the reading of the Gospels, which are the four books that record the words and deeds of Jesus. In doing this we acknowledge that the living Word of God has entered the room, so it is only right to stand, if one is able to do so. We also rise for the Nicene Creed, a 1,600-year-old statement of our beliefs. And we most often stand to sing (although it is not rare to sing some more meditative music, such as the Psalms or communion hymns while seated).

When we sit, we do so to convey our readiness to learn, as we (were supposed to) do at school. We sit to listen to the Old and New Testament lessons as well as taking part in the Psalm, and for the sermon.

Referred to by some as "pew aerobics," our penchant for communal participation comes from a shared belief that Sunday worship is not a spectator sport. Kneeling, sitting, and standing are all about inspiring us to say thanks together, the very best way we know how.

Of course, not all people are able to join in these various postures of prayer and praise, and it is important to be sensitive to those who are unable to do so. Posture is there to assist us in focusing our hearts and minds, not to establish righteousness.

About the Anglican Slump

This is a form of semi-kneeling that has begun to die out as the amount of time spent kneeling has been reduced in recent years. It consists of placing one's knees on the kneeler but resting one's posterior on the edge of the pew.

WHY SOME EPISCOPALIANS BOW AND CROSS THEMSELVES (AND WHY SOME DON'T)

Roman Catholics and Latino-American baseball players aren't the only ones. Many Episcopalians are also in the habit of practicing an ancient body prayer: making the sign of the cross. This is typically done when beginning and ending prayers and ceremonies. It's also a stand-alone practice of asking God to bless oneself.

To many Episcopalians, making the sign of the cross is a humble, silent prayer used to remind us of Christ's sacrifice and also the cross we are called to bear. The cross was an instrument of cruel punishment and a symbol of horror. Through the suffering and death of Christ, it became the sign of victory over evil and of life over death. Many people believe we do well to remind ourselves of this as often as possible.

Some Episcopalians don't agree. Some believe it's ostentatious and superfluous. Of course, no one is required to make such actions— or to judge those who do or do not.

There are no hard-and-fast rules regarding such body prayers in the Episcopal Church. Some people genuflect ("bend the knee") or bow at the mention of the name of Jesus Christ, before approaching the altar, or when the processional cross goes by. Others don't. These are personal acts of piety and are completely optional. Bottom line: if it's for you, join in; if not, don't.

That said, here's how many Episcopalians cross themselves:

1. Touch the fingertips of your right hand to your forehead. Say to yourself, "In the Name of the Father . . ."

2. Touch your chest. Say, "and of the Son . . ."

3. Touch the front side of your left shoulder. Say, "and of the Holy . . ."

4. Touch your right shoulder in roughly the same location. Say, "Spirit."

5. Return your hand to your heart, or to your side, or join your hands and say "Amen."

At the Beginning of the Gospel

As the minister announces the reading of the Gospel, many Episcopalians make three small crosses with their thumb at the forehead, lips, and heart. This represents a desire to consecrate mind, deed, and will to God, preparing to hear the words of the Gospel afresh and ready to respond.

Other Times People Use This Action

As a matter of personal piety, some people make the sign of the cross before or after receiving communion, during the Eucharistic prayer at the petition for God to bless and sanctify us, and at the end of the Creed. As we said above, it is all up to you.

HOW TO SHARE THE PEACE

In Romans 16:16, Paul tells members of the congregation to "greet one another with a holy kiss." The First Letter of Peter ends, "Greet one another with a kiss of love. Peace to all of you who are in Christ" (1 Peter 5:14).

Some Episcopalians worry about this part of the liturgy, which can range from a polite exchange of nods or handshakes to a noisy few minutes as people leave their pews and try to greet everyone else with a hug. Some people feel uncomfortable or dislike being hugged or hugging others. You can survive the peace, however, with these steps.

Adopt a peaceful frame of mind. Clear your mind of distracting and disrupting thoughts so you can participate joyfully and reverently.

Determine the form of contact with which you feel comfortable, your "safe touch." Handshaking is most common. Be prepared, however, for hugs, half-hugs, one-armed hugs, pats, and other forms of physical contact. Nods are appropriate for distances greater than two pews or rows.

Try to refrain from extended conversation. The sharing of the peace is not the best time for lengthy introductions to new people, comments about the weather, observations about yesterday's game, or swapping recipes. A brief encounter is appropriate, but save conversation for the after-worship coffee hour.

Make appropriate eye contact. Look the other person in the eye but avoid staring. The action of looking the person in the eye highlights the relationship brothers and sisters in Christ have with one another.

Declare the peace of God. "The peace of the Lord be with you," "Peace be with you," "The peace of God," "God's peace," and "The

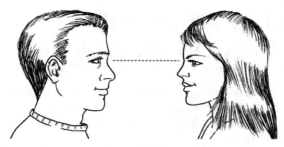

Make good eye contact as you share God's peace with others.

peace of Christ" are among common ways of speaking the peace. Once spoken, the peace is there. Move on to the next person.

Be Aware

Safe touch involves contact that occurs within your personal space but does not cause discomfort or unease. Respect others as you expect them to respect you.

WHAT IS THE BOOK
OF COMMON PRAYER?

When King Henry VIII separated the Church of England from the authority of the Roman Catholic Church by the Act of Supremacy in 1534, it became necessary to revise the Church's worship to reflect the change.

Henry told Archbishop Thomas Cranmer that he wanted all liturgical books "newly examined, corrected, reformed, and castigated, from all manner of mention of the Bishop of Rome's name, from all apocryphas, feigned legends, superstitions, orations, collects, versicles, and responses; that the names and memories of all saints which be not mentioned in the Scripture or authentic doctors should be abolished, and put out of the same books and calendars, and that the service should be made out of the Scripture and other authentic doctors."

In 1544, Cranmer was ordered to prepare a general supplication "in our native English tongue," to be "continually from henceforth said and sung in all churches of our realm with such reverence and devotion as appertaineth." A new "Order of the Communion" passed Parliament in 1548, and the next year Parliament's "Act for Uniformity of Service and Administration of the Sacraments throughout the Realm" established "The Book of Common Prayer, and Administration of the Sacraments, and other Rites and Ceremonies of the Church, after the Use of the Church of England" as the official worship book for the Church. This, and all subsequent editions and adaptations, including the one used by Episcopalians, is often referred to simply as "the BCP."

The English 1549 edition went through revisions in 1552 and 1559 before its present English form, the 1662 version. It remains an official Book of Common Prayer for the Church of England, recently supplemented with a multi-volume library called *Common Worship*.

Churches that trace their origin to the Church of England have often revised and produced Prayer Books of their own to reflect their national or local circumstances and languages. The Episcopal Church separated from the Church of England at the time of the American Revolution and published its first Book of Common Prayer, based on both English and Scottish sources. Further revisions to the American book were made in 1892, 1928, and most extensively in 1979. It has also been translated into a number of languages, as there are a number of non-English-speaking congregations in the Episcopal Church, not only in its overseas branches, but in many parts of the United States.

Each revision saw some controversy and opposition, although as Cranmer himself said in the preface to his own efforts: "There was never anything by the wit of man so well devised, or so sure established, which in continuance of time hath not been corrupted," so continuing revision is a part of the Church's communal task.

Two Prefaces

The 1979 Book of Common Prayer includes the texts both of Cranmer's 1549 Preface (page 866) and the preface to the first American edition of 1789 (page 9). Both of them lay out the rationale for revision, and reveal some of the thinking of the revisers.

WHY DO EPISCOPALIANS READ THEIR PRAYERS?

When the disciples came to Jesus and asked him how they should pray, he offered them a specific form of prayer that we call the "Our Father" or "The Lord's Prayer."

Episcopalians, like many Christians, believe that when we write our prayers down we carry forward an ancient tradition of order and structure suggested in Jesus' instructions to the disciples. There is nothing new in that; one of the biggest collections of prayers still in use is the Book of Psalms.

When we think about it, even the most laid-back, contemporary liturgies rely on some written, pre-arranged format. There's the bulletin (or the projected texts), the songs, and of course the sermon outline, if not the entire sermon text. While there is a danger if written prayers become hollow and repetitious—something Jesus warned against—written prayers have a lot to offer, including, perhaps most importantly, the possibility of *common* prayer. And let's face it, impromptu or improvised prayer can also be hollow and repetitious.

Episcopalians find that *common* prayer allows us to partake more deeply in a shared experience of offering something we agree on, and recite together. Most of our prayers have stood the test of time regarding the beliefs they express and the clarity with which they state them. When we pray them, we are uniting not just with each other but with generations of believers who have prayed the same prayers. Just think of the billions of people who have prayed the Our Father, the Agnus Dei ("Lamb of God . . .") or the Sanctus ("Holy, holy, holy . . ."), or the 23rd Psalm.

Think of a written prayer as the refrain to your favorite song. That song may be several years old and you may have sung it hundreds of times. But that doesn't make it any less touching or enjoyable. Good songs age well, and so do good prayers.

About the Collect

Prayer is also not only *in* the spoken repetition of those written words—it is also in our silent and inward reflection *on* those words.

One of the most characteristic prayer forms in the Episcopal tradition is the collect. (A note on pronunciation: as with many a noun spelled the same as a verb, the noun gets an accent on the first, rather than last, syllable: KAW-lekt.) This is a prayer that comes at the end of a longer period of particular intentions, said aloud or prayed silently, often with periods of silence interspersed or at the end. It is normally said by the officiant, and it is meant to *collect* all of the other prayers and offer a final dedication of them to God, usually "through Jesus Christ our Lord." The people's "Amen" at the end is their assent and agreement, and means, "So be it" or "Truly!" Think of all the preceding prayers said silently or aloud as a bouquet being gathered together and presented at the end.

HOW TO LISTEN TO A SERMON

Episcopalians believe God's Word comes to us through worship and the proclamation of Holy Scripture. Honoring God's Word, not to mention getting something out of worship, includes engaged listening to the sermon and active mental participation.

Review active listening skills. Even though the listener in this case doesn't usually get to speak, the sermon is still a conversation. Make mental notes as you listen. Take notice of where and why you react and which emotions you experience or what thoughts arise.

Take notes. Note-taking promotes active listening and provides a good basis for later reflection. It also allows you to return to confusing or complicated parts at your own leisure, or to ask the preacher what she or he meant. Some congregations provide space in the bulletin for notes.

Maintain your posture while remaining comfortable. Sit upright with your feet on the floor. Beware of the impulse to slouch, cross your arms, or lean against your neighbor, as these can encourage drowsiness.

Listen for the Gospel. This is the "good news" that should be at the heart of any good sermon. Upon hearing this news, you may feel a sense of gratitude, as though you've set down a burden. You may find your emotions moved or stirred. This is normal.

End by saying "Amen." Since preaching is mostly God's work, honor the Word by sealing the moment with this sacred word affirming what you have heard.

Review. If you've taken written notes, read through them later that day or the next day and consider conversing with the preacher if you have questions or need clarification. If you've taken mental notes, review them in a quiet moment. Consider sharing this review time with others in your congregation or household on a weekly basis. Some parishes have regular Bible study to reexamine the Scripture passages heard that day, and the sermon.

HOW TO PASS THE PLATE

Passing the offering plate requires physical flexibility and an ability to adapt to differing practices. The offering is a practice that dates back to Old Testament times, linking money and personal finance directly to one's identity as a child of God. Giving of one's financial resources is an integral part of a healthy faith life.

Pay attention to instructions, if any are given. The officiant may announce the method of offering, or instructions may be printed in the worship bulletin.

Be prepared—have your offering ready prior to worship. Many churches use an envelope system for regular members, but may also provide blank envelopes for visitors and newcomers. Often these can be used to record your name or indicate your interest in joining the congregation.

Be aware of different plate or basket types. Some congregations use wide-rimmed, flat, felt-lined, metal or wooden offering plates. Some use baskets of varying types. Some use cloth bags on the ends of long wooden poles that the ushers extend inward from the ends of the pews. Don't be too surprised to have something unusual poked under your nose!

Be alert to the offering plate or basket's arrival at your row. Keep an eye on the ushers, if there are any. In most congregations, guiding the offering is part of their ministry, so wherever they are, so is the plate. As the plate approaches you, set aside other activity and prepare for passing.

Focus on your own gift rather than your neighbor's offering. Many people contribute once a month by mail and some by automatic withdrawal from a bank account. If your neighbor passes the plate to you without placing an envelope, check, or cash in it, do not assume they didn't contribute in some other way.

Place your offering in the plate and pass it to the next person, following the usher's instructions. Do not attempt to make change from the plate if your offering is in cash. Avoid letting the plate rest in your lap as you finish writing a check. (This is why we suggested being prepared prior to worship!)

Be Aware

- Some congregations place the offering plate or basket at the rear of the worship space, for worshipers to make an offering as they enter, rather than having a "collection." Some do both.
- Your church offering may be tax deductible, as provided by law. Consider making your offering by check or automatic withdrawal; you will receive a statement from your church in the first quarter of the next year.
- Churches often depend entirely upon the funds that come through congregational offerings. If you are a member, resolve to work yourself toward tithing as a putting-your-money-where-your-mouth-is expression of faith. (The term tithing means "one-tenth" and refers to the practice of giving 10 percent of one's income to support the church's work. This is widely considered a good standard of Christian giving.)
- Everyone, regardless of age, has something to offer.
- Offerings are not fees or dues given merely out of obligation. They are gifts of thanksgiving returned to God from the heart, as well as the diligent performance of a duty to support the work of the church.

HOW MUCH MONEY SHOULD I PUT INTO THE OFFERING PLATE?

As with most churches, Episcopal congregations rely on donations from members for most of their operating expenses, as well as major capital expenditures.

Once a year many congregations hold a "stewardship" or "pledge campaign," asking each individual or family to make a financial commitment for the upcoming year. The leadership then total those promises to create a budget.

In general, Episcopal congregations spend much of their income on salaries, building maintenance (including utilities and insurance), programming, and outreach. Since the first two tend to be fixed costs, the more that is collected, the more a church's ministry and mission can be expanded into new programs for those outside the parish.

Of course, donations also come in the form of volunteer time. For example, electricians help with maintenance and accountants help keep the books, offsetting what otherwise might be a major expense.

However, the main reason for giving to a church has less to do with paying bills and much more to do with cultivating generous hearts. God wants us to be generous (2 Corinthians 9:7). The Lord wants us to be known not by the kind of car we drive, the size of the house we live in, or the jewelry we wear, but by our love. As Christ gave himself for us, so too are we asked to give of ourselves for others. The old adage "Give 'til it hurts" comes to mind—but it could be better phrased as "give 'til it *heals*."

That's why the Episcopal Church suggests its members use the tithe (10 percent of one's income) as a starting point. Most parishes gratefully receive any contribution. However, how we handle our possessions is a spiritual issue and our churches address it by gently challenging their members to grow—to strive less for acquiring things for ourselves, and doing more in sharing in those things that benefit the whole community, including the church and its outreach.

WHY IS THE ALTAR BIGGER THAN THE PULPIT (OR VICE VERSA)?

Church interiors offer more clues than a crime scene on a TV forensic drama.

Every banner, color, symbol, and piece of furnishing gives us an indication as to what goes on in that space, and what the people believe who call that space home. This is especially true when it comes to the size and placement of altars and pulpits in Episcopal churches.

Early Christians divided their Sunday worship into two parts, concentrating respectively on Word and Sacrament. This continues today in Episcopal liturgies (a trait shared by most "liturgical" churches). That means during the first part of the worship we hear Bible readings, usually selections from the Hebrew Scripture (or from the Book of Acts during Easter Season), the Psalms, the New Testament Epistles, and one of the Gospels. This is followed by the sermon, the proclamation of faith (the Creed), and the prayers. The Prayer Book commends the pulpit as an appropriate place from which to proclaim and preach. Some churches divide readings and preaching between a lectern and a pulpit, and may proclaim the gospel from the aisle, in the midst of the assembled congregation.

The second part of the liturgy revolves around the Holy Communion. The celebrant leads a special prayer called the Eucharistic Prayer, and all focus is drawn to the altar and the reminder of Christ's gift of himself for us. The drama reaches a pinnacle when the bread is broken at the altar and offered to the people with the words, "The Gifts of God for the People of God."

Naturally, it is difficult to put equal weights on these two parts. Some congregations tend to put greater emphasis on the reading and exposition of Scripture—this explains congregations with large and prominent pulpits. Other congregations tend to focus on the presence and mystery of Christ in the Eucharist, and have larger altar areas, in addition to making use of incense, bells, and more ornate clergy vestments.

A Note on Altitude

You may encounter the terms High Church and Low Church, though they are somewhat less common than they were in the nineteenth and twentieth centuries. These reflect the style of worship, including how the clergy are vested, and whether incense is used (or not). However, many particulars once considered "High" (such as the use of candles at the altar, or the use of vestments other than cassock and surplice) have long since become mainstream.

Other terms you may encounter are "Anglo-Catholic" and "Evangelical." These concern more than just the worship style, although the differing emphasis of each tradition is reflected in the worship. While many churches fall somewhere in between, those that don't are usually quite happy to identify themselves as High, Low, Anglo-Catholic, or Evangelical. In most cases it is a question of style and emphasis, rather than content. The Gospel is ultimately the Gospel.

WHY IS THAT EMPTY CHAIR NEAR THE ALTAR?

No matter how full an Episcopal church may be on Sunday, chances are no one will be sitting in one specific chair located somewhere near the altar.

This special seat is a sign and a symbol of the unity and authority that comes from the particular way Episcopalians have of organizing themselves: it's the bishop's chair.

The Episcopal Church believes in bishops, those among us who are called to a particular aspect of church leadership. In fact, the word "Episcopal" derives from the Greek word for "bishop" (*episkopos,* which literally means "overseer" or "supervisor"). Diocesan bishops are the senior pastors of the church in a particular geographical area called a *diocese.* The bishop is the spiritual pastor for the area, which is why he or she may carry a shepherd's staff called a *crozier.* The bishop exercises this ministry mainly through the priests and deacons, who serve the smaller geographic areas called parishes.

A bishop has one main seat; its Greek name is *cathedra.* This is where we get the word *cathedral,* literally the place where the bishop is seated. However, bishops get out a lot, regularly visiting parishes, which is why they have a seat reserved. This is a reminder not only of the authority of the bishop, but of the congregation's relationship with the bishop. The empty chair is a reminder to pray for and with our bishop.

Other Flavors of Bishops

The **diocesan** bishop is a singular character, and any diocese can have only one (at a time). But often there are other bishops who function in accord with the church's rules (the Constitution and Canons).

A bishop who intends to retire may request the election of a **coadjutor** whose ministry as bishop will overlap with the diocesan's in a carefully spelled out division of labor and on-the-job training. When the diocesan retires, the coadjutor becomes diocesan.

Some larger dioceses with many parishes find it helpful to have a **suffragan** bishop who is elected to serve along with the diocesan, usually with a defined portfolio of responsibilities in addition to parish visitation.

In some cases a diocese may contract with a bishop who has resigned from another diocese to serve as an **assistant** bishop.

Finally a bishop who has retired may also be on call to help out as an **assisting** bishop in the area in which he or she lives.

TELLING THE SEASON OF THE YEAR BY THE COLOR OF THE ALTAR HANGINGS

Episcopal worship is color-coded, although this is a matter of tradition and not a requirement.

Like other liturgical churches, the Episcopal Church upholds the long tradition of arranging the year around the life of Jesus Christ.

It all begins with Advent (violet or blue), the season at the start of the Christian year, which is a four-week countdown to Jesus' birthday, the Nativity or Christmas (white). We celebrate the Incarnation for 12 days before Epiphany (hence the famous carol, "On the first day of Christmas my true love gave to me . . ."). Epiphany commemorates the coming of the Three Kings, and the season after it (green) lasts until Ash Wednesday, the first day of Lent (violet again, or in some places unbleached linen). Because Lent starts 40 days before Easter (not counting Sundays), the date of Ash Wednesday will differ from year to year. That's because, as everybody knows, Easter falls on the first Sunday after the first full moon after the vernal equinox, the first day of spring. (What, you didn't know that?) Lent leads us to Holy Week (blood red or purple), which includes the Great Three Days: Maundy Thursday (which can change to white for the commemoration of the founding of the Holy Eucharist), Good Friday (back to blood red, purple, or even black), and Holy Saturday (also blood red or purple). That Saturday evening marks the Easter Vigil, and then Easter Day itself, the biggest holy day of them all, which is why we spend the next 50 days partying (and wearing white). Then we hit the day of Pentecost (red), the day the Holy Spirit came down on Jesus' disciples, and then we're off on the long "green season" studying the teachings and miracles of Jesus.

If you found this hard to follow, then you know why there are colors to each season, which are often displayed in hangings on the pulpit and lectern, the altar, and the clergy vestments.

THE SEASONS OF
THE CHURCH YEAR

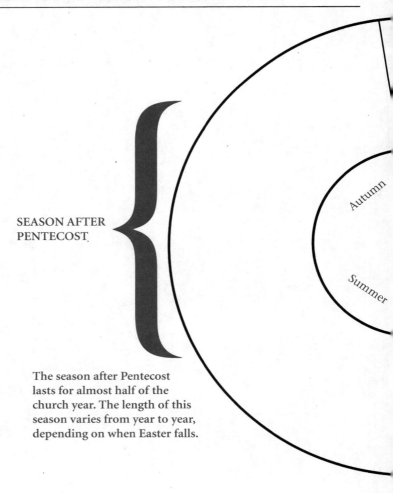

SEASON AFTER
PENTECOST

The season after Pentecost
lasts for almost half of the
church year. The length of this
season varies from year to year,
depending on when Easter falls.

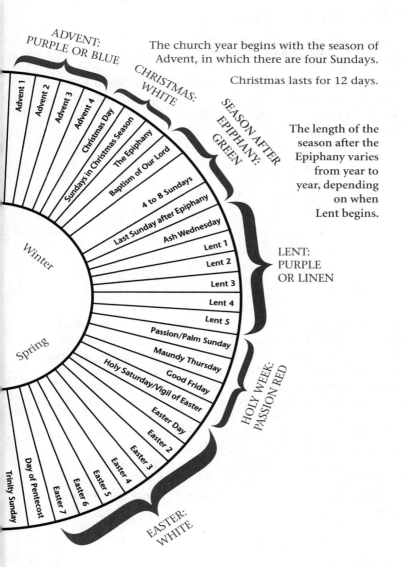

The church year begins with the season of Advent, in which there are four Sundays.

Christmas lasts for 12 days.

The length of the season after the Epiphany varies from year to year, depending on when Lent begins.

ADVENT: PURPLE OR BLUE

CHRISTMAS: WHITE

SEASON AFTER EPIPHANY: GREEN

LENT: PURPLE OR LINEN

HOLY WEEK: PASSION RED

EASTER: WHITE

Advent 1
Advent 2
Advent 3
Advent 4
Christmas Day
Sundays in Christmas Season
The Epiphany
Baptism of Our Lord
4 to 8 Sundays
Last Sunday after Epiphany
Ash Wednesday
Lent 1
Lent 2
Lent 3
Lent 4
Lent 5
Passion/Palm Sunday
Maundy Thursday
Good Friday
Holy Saturday/Vigil of Easter
Easter Day
Easter 2
Easter 3
Easter 4
Easter 5
Easter 6
Easter 7
Day of Pentecost
Trinity Sunday

Winter

Spring

WHY ALL THE STAINED GLASS?

Formed by two of the world's most basic elements, earth and fire, it is no wonder that Christians have long seen glass in churches as a window to more than just the outside.

No one knows who invented stained glass (it may have started with jewelry) but its popularity began spreading in the Middle Ages during the European church and cathedral building boom. Advances in architecture allowed for large, sweeping windows, and many church designers used them to say something big about God. Medieval craftspeople believed they were building sacred spaces to give glory to God, and to instruct the people in the history and mystery of the faith. They were interested in creating an atmosphere of grandeur where people could sense God's presence. They also knew that a picture is worth 1,000 words, and often portrayed incidents from the Bible in their windows. Thus, early stained glass windows were to be experienced both for their beauty and their message.

Stained glass windows in churches often depict a biblical scene, a sacrament, a famous saint, or some aspect of natural wonder that reveals the power and majesty of God. Such windows maintain effectiveness as teaching tools. Think of stained glass windows as the medieval church's PowerPoint. They helped new Christians learn Bible stories and reminded older members of their sacred story.

The idea behind stained glass, and many furnishings in Episcopal churches, is that the presence of beautiful objects can lift our souls closer to God. Like nature, stained glass windows open our eyes to the wonders of God. They remind us of our past and point us to the future. When we look at stained glass we see God's story played out in myriad different levels. And when we think about it, that's really not a bad way to look out at the world.

Other Visual Arts

Other visual aids are often found in Episcopal churches, including mural paintings, statuary and relief carvings, and fabric art such as weavings and banners. In recent years there has been a resurgence of interest in icons, long a part of the Eastern Orthodox tradition.

To get a taste of the wide range of art Episcopalians have produced, from photography to macramé, pay a visit to the website of the Episcopal Church and the Visual Arts (*ecva.org*).

DO EPISCOPALIANS BELIEVE IN SAINTS?

Of course they do; but, as with most things, it depends on how you define *believe* and *saints*. All Christians are part of the Communion of Saints, both the living and the dead. In part, because of this solidarity or communion, how we treat the saints who have gone before differs from the way in which saints are treated in some other traditions. Some religious traditions more or less ignore the departed saints; others invoke them in prayer. The Anglican position, spelled out in Article XXII of the Articles of Religion (see BCP 872) rejected the "invocation of saints"—that is, asking the saints to pray for us. Even though that was the official policy in the days of the Reformation, many Episcopalians have come to see asking for the prayers of the saints to be much like asking a friend to say a prayer for you. Still, the Prayer Book does not contain any official forms by which a saint or saints are asked for prayer (usually understood as "invocation") but does recognize that the saints in glory pray and praise God (see the introduction to "Holy, Holy, Holy," page 402, and more specifically the second prayer on page 504). We join them in that prayer and praise.

More importantly, Episcopalians commemorate the feast days (usually the date of death or "spiritual birthday") of Christians whose lives and deeds have been exemplary. These include Martin Luther King, Jr., William Wilberforce, and Elizabeth Cady Stanton. Liturgies for celebrating those feasts may be found in *Lesser Feasts and Fasts* and in *Holy Women, Holy Men,* authorized for trial use by the General Convention in 2009, and published in 2010. These volumes contain biographies of and liturgical texts for many men and women the Church wishes to honor and commend for their example. In high-altitude Anglo-Catholic churches, prayers addressing the Virgin Mary and other saints are not unknown. There is a formal process by which commemorations of such faithful souls can be added to the calendar of the BCP. This process is spelled out in *Lesser Feasts and Fasts* and *Holy Women, Holy Men*. This latter volume included many more provisional additions to the calendar, and revision continues.

WHY EPISCOPALIANS DRESS UP (ESPECIALLY THE CLERGY)

When you meet the president, you wear a tie.

When you go to your prom, you rent a tux.

When you get married, you break out the gown.

Let's face it, the most conspicuous way we show respect, or mark a special occasion, is with wardrobe.

And that's the biggest reason many Episcopalians tend to dress up for worship.

Episcopalians like to think that our Sunday morning worship commends an elevated sense of respect and honor, our "Sunday best." Sure, we're meeting one another, our close friends and family, but we are also meeting the Lord. And the Bible tells us that entry onto holy ground has, among other things, caused some people to remove their shoes. So we may be getting off easy with a simple suit coat.

Clergy usually lead the fashion parade. The bright colors, intricate patterns, and high-quality fabrics worn by many clergy are intended to impart a level of formality that is festive yet serious. Clergy remind us of our core beliefs; that Christ is present in the Word proclaimed, in the gathered community (Jesus says, "wherever two or more are gathered in my name, I am present"), and in Holy Communion ("This is my body, this is my blood"). And if Christ is really present, then one way we recognize this is by dressing up.

In our increasingly casual environment this is, admittedly, a hard sell.

We realize we're counter-cultural.

We know that lots of people might not see things this way. Heck, not even all Episcopalians dress up for worship.

But that's OK. We know that no matter how people dress, Jesus shows up at millions of different churches on Sundays. Some of us just like to have our shoes polished when he comes.

About Those Vestments

The glossary on page 202 lists a number of the vestments commonly worn by clergy, but we wanted to highlight the most basic here. You are likely to see these in most Episcopal churches.

The **alb** is a white gown with long sleeves that covers any street clothes worn underneath. It is a reminder of the white baptismal garment of the early church, and it is often worn by all of the ministers taking part in worship, including acolytes and altar servers. In this way it serves as a literal "uniform."

The **stole** is a narrow band of cloth, usually ornamented, that symbolizes the office of ministry. Deacons, priests, and bishops all normally wear a stole as part of their liturgical outfit. Deacons usually wear the stole over one shoulder and across the chest, while priests and bishops wear the stole around the neck, either crossed in front or hanging straight down. The stole is often tucked into loops in the **cincture**, a rope tied around the waist.

The **chasuble** is an outer garment similar to a poncho, usually made of fine fabric and sometimes highly decorated. It is usually worn by the celebrant.

DO EPISCOPALIANS LEAVE CHURCH EARLY?

It's not that we can't, it's just that we—don't.

Chalk it up to our proper English heritage, but few people seem to make a motion for the door until the last line of the last hymn is completed, and the deacon or priest gives the formal dismissal. Even then, some will remain for a time of quiet prayer, or to listen to a musical postlude. In some parishes there is a tradition—whose roots defy discovery—of waiting until all altar candles have been extinguished before anyone makes a move.

Episcopalians owe much to our deferential Anglican roots. As we know, all churches have a distinctive culture, or DNA. Some of our proclivities are seen in:

- the polite distance we tend to give visitors;
- our hesitancy to talk about money;
- our aversion to any kind of pushy hard-sell that would make someone feel uncomfortable;

- the particular gusto with which we sing hymns;
- our desire to stick around until our worship is officially over—and often longer!

The formality of much Episcopal worship is not intended to constrict; rather, it grows out of an understanding that boundaries aren't a bad thing—that games are actually better played when they have rules. Of course, that's not to say our rules are any better than anyone else's. But it is to say that we have them, and that the best way to learn them is by joining in. And you're invited to show up next Sunday for practice. After all, that's what people mean when they say they are "practicing Christians."

IS COFFEE HOUR REALLY ANOTHER SACRAMENT?

No, but it is certainly a regular feature in most Episcopal congregations.

Not content just to remain in the worship space for a while after the worship has ended, following the main Sunday worship at many Episcopal churches you may find a gathering with a highly creative name: Coffee Hour. As if the title doesn't give it away, this is an informal get-together of parish friends and family to catch up over a cup of coffee and warm conversation.

The importance of these gatherings cannot be overestimated. Most Episcopal congregations are relatively small (average attendance is under a hundred on Sunday morning) and include generations of extended families. These people are godparents to each other's children, Sunday School teachers, choir members, leaders on youth outings, etc. Given the depth of relationship, it is easy to understand why Coffee Hour is so important.

Of course this can make it difficult for a visitor to break in, and the best advice is patience. Or better yet: introduce yourself. As with family reunions, Coffee Hour can lead to clusters of folks with mutually familiar faces, and the newcomer can be unintentionally overlooked, or made to feel more a stranger than she is.

Coffee also plays an important part in the life of many parishes. Many Episcopal churches offer space for use by 12-step recovery programs whose life-blood tends to be coffee.

By the way, Episcopalians officially recognize two sacraments, Baptism and Holy Communion, as given to us by Jesus in the Gospel. Five other sacramental rites are regularly part of our worship life: Confirmation, Ordination, Holy Matrimony, Reconciliation of a Penitent (sometimes called Confession), and Unction (anointing of the sick). Coffee Hour is unlikely to make the cut.

HOW TO JOIN AN EPISCOPAL CHURCH

Just show up.

OK, this may not be the only requirement, but it is, by far, the most important, and it's the first step.

Some Episcopal parishes are intentionally vague about assigning membership. We definitely don't want to be known as places where your membership is assigned only if you pass muster. We are much less concerned about counting the people who are in, than we are about leaving someone out.

You can consult your local parish for details, but what's specified by the Episcopal Church's Constitution and Canons governs all congregations. If you have been baptized, letting the clergy in charge of the congregation know, so that the information can be recorded, makes you a **member**. (If you were already a member of a different Episcopal church, the clergy person will let the other church know so that your name can be transferred.)

If you or members of your family have never been baptized, speak to the clergy person and find out what procedures the congregation uses to prepare people for baptism. This will vary considerably depending on the size of the congregation and its resources.

Members of the church who receive communion at least three times a year are considered **communicants.** (This rule goes back to a time when communion was much less frequent than it is now. In the early years there were congregations that only had communion four times a year; now almost all congregations have communion at least twice a month and more likely every Sunday.)

Communicants who, as the canon states, "have been faithful in corporate worship . . . and have been faithful in working, praying, and giving for the spread of the Kingdom of God, are to be considered **communicants in good standing**."

Being a member of an Episcopal congregation means a connection with the bishop, so it is expected that all Episcopalians will at some point have made an adult affirmation of their faith in the presence of the bishop. This can take the form of confirmation, reception, or reaffirmation.

We believe the church should reflect the open and accepting arms of Jesus. The canonical legalities play second fiddle to the importance of a particular faith community in one's life: Is this particular church "home"? If so (and we hope it is), you're in.

And, keep showing up!

HOW TO GET MARRIED IN AN EPISCOPAL CHURCH

They're a Hollywood location scout's dream.

Many Episcopal parishes make idyllic backdrops for couples to make some of the most important promises of their lives. The traditional architecture, polished brass, and timeworn pews all contribute to the demand for weddings that some parishes experience. And most are very happy to accommodate starry-eyed couples.

Of course, marriage is not built on buildings. It's built on people who make commitments. And the Episcopal Church wants to make sure that every marriage has the very best chance of succeeding, and that the "church wedding" have more connection with the Church than just the venue. The BCP requires that at least the bride or groom be baptized. Time is needed before the wedding for proper pre-marital counseling. There are also county and state requirements that need to be satisfied in order for weddings to happen, as the clergy person is normally functioning both as a minister of the church and an agent of the state.

Episcopalians love marriage. We see it as an earthly representation of the mysterious union between Christ and the church. The love of two people that leads them toward life-long commitment to one another reflects God's commitment always to be by our side. And since God accepts all of us, some parishes also bless the unions (or in some states marriages) of same-sex couples, in which we can see the virtues of fidelity, affection, respect, and love. So the bottom line is, if you'd like to get married in an Episcopal church, contact the parish you're interested in and ask about their particular guidelines. They differ from place to place, but each is intended to help the marriage succeed and flourish.

HOW TO GET RE-MARRIED
IN AN EPISCOPAL CHURCH

For a church whose heritage includes the oft-married Henry VIII, you'd think we'd be good at this one. But the fact is, divorce is rarely good; it is difficult, painful, even if sometimes the best option available. As one wise Episcopal priest once said, "Marriages are living things; and sometimes they die." We recognize that reality.

The Episcopal Church sees a marriage as a human endeavor, almost always entered into with good intentions. But, like everything else we attempt, we can fail no matter how hard we try. When marriages fail, we believe the best place to go to put lives back together is the church. Divorced people are welcome at our churches and at our communion rail. The counsel of clergy and the friendship of parishioners have helped countless people through this agonizing experience.

However, once a divorce has occurred and remarriage becomes a possibility, there are considerations to keep in mind. These have to do with taking care of the responsibilities arising out of the previous relationship, including the well-being of the former spouse and any children from that prior marriage. The overriding concerns have to do with responsibility, honesty, and integrity. Divorce and remarriage are intimate affairs and best left to the counsel of your local Episcopal clergy person, who would be happy to answer any questions.

Because the permission of the bishop is required for the marriage of a divorced person whose former spouse is still living, checking with the clergy in a timely manner is very important, as some bishops require significant lead time and information in order to make their decision on permitting the cleric to solemnize the marriage.

It is within the discretion of the cleric to decline to solemnize any given marriage. In short, Episcopalians take marriage seriously.

HOW TO ENROLL YOUR CHILD IN SUNDAY SCHOOL

Just as Jesus beckoned children to come to him (Matthew 19:13), so does the church.

Episcopal congregations usually offer a variety of Sunday School and Christian educational programming, for children and adults. (Much will depend on the size and resources of the parish.) Some of the more popular (and worth Googling) programs for children are the Catechesis of the Good Shepherd, Godly Play, Worship Center, Journey to Adulthood, and Weaving God's Promises. The Episcopal Church asks that Sunday school teachers be screened and have special "Safe Church" training in sexual misconduct awareness. Children are God's gift to parents and to churches and we do the best we can to safeguard our young ones.

Because Episcopal parishes tend to be small, class sizes are small too, which provides a better student–teacher ratio. Classes are offered at most parishes throughout the school year (September–May) but may also include Vacation Bible School, summer mission trips, and pilgrimages.

Since the Episcopal Church does not believe that young people are the "future" of the church—they *are* the church—we welcome their participation in various leadership capacities. They are also encouraged to take leadership roles in various diocesan, provincial, and national church activities.

If you are interested in finding out what's offered at your local Episcopal parish, give them a call. If you want to find a parish close to you, go to *theredbook.org.*

HOW TO BECOME A CHRISTIAN

To most Episcopalians, this is a puzzling question.

That's because many of us were baptized as children and raised in Christian homes. Many of us have never not known what it is like to be a Christian. This is common among Christians in liturgical churches. For Episcopalians, as for most Christians, baptism is what makes you a Christian—a member of the Body of Christ (whether you are an Episcopalian or not!).

On the other end of the spectrum are faith communities that constantly ask and explain what it is to "come to Jesus." This "revival" approach can be particularly appealing to people, but it muddies the baptismal water a bit, risking making "being a Christian" more about how one feels.

From the Episcopal point of view, becoming a Christian is, and is not, difficult. Obviously, in the case of an infant, baptism is not about personal choice, though the sponsors do make some serious promises on the child's behalf. For such sponsors, and for those baptized as adults, the "easy" part is saying the words by which we renounce our sins, turn to Christ as savior, and pledge to repent when we sin. The hard part is actually doing it.

Episcopalians use the words of our Baptismal Covenant (BCP 304, and page 222 of this book). Not only is this recited at all baptisms, but it is often used on several Sundays a year even when there are no candidates to be baptized. This "renewal" may be our own form of "revival" as we recognize the importance of reminding ourselves of our pledge to follow Christ. We nurture it by coming to church regularly, partaking of Holy Communion, and praying frequently.

If you are interested in becoming a Christian, read the Baptismal Covenant, talk to an Episcopalian, or contact your local Episcopal clergy person.

WHAT TO SAY AT A VIEWING OR AFTER A FUNERAL

Episcopalians are not a demonstrative people, by and large, and so the viewing (also called a vigil, wake, or watch) and the funeral in the Episcopal tradition are often restrained and serious. The Book of Common Prayer offers a brief liturgy of "Prayers for a Vigil" (page 465), and additional prayers are available in *Enriching Our Worship 2*. The focus of the burial liturgy itself is on the hope of the Resurrection, but rarely are the bereaved quite ready to hear that from anyone save the clergy. In conversation with those suffering the pain of such loss, simplicity and judicious honesty are best.

Do say:

I am so sorry for your loss.

[Name of deceased] was a good person. S/he will be missed.

I have never been through something like this and can only imagine what you feel, but please know that I am praying for you.

What do you need right now? How can I help?

I am here to listen whenever you are ready.

Please accept my deepest sympathy to you and your family.

Unhelpful and wisely avoided:

Only the good die young.

God must have needed another angel/needed him more than we do.

You'll find someone else (or, you'll have other children). Don't worry. You'll see him/her again.

At least s/he didn't suffer long.

S/he is in a better place.

Be thankful s/he doesn't have to experience pain and heartache on this earth any more.

Doesn't s/he look natural?

And remember, silence and a gentle look or gesture can sometimes be more eloquent than any words.

WHY MORE PEOPLE DON'T GO TO CHURCH

Actually, a fair number of Americans do. The Gallup Organization and Pew Research have been measuring church attendance for years, and find that Americans, year after year, self-report a significant church-going rate on any given Sunday. Due to flaws in self-reporting (Americans typically say they vote more than they do and say they visit questionable websites much less than they do), this number is probably much smaller, perhaps 25 to 30 percent, which is still a sizable number.

However, more than three-quarters of Americans identify themselves as Christians. Most Americans say they believe in God and are spiritual people. So what keeps them from joining a church? Why the gap of about two-to-one between belief and practice?

Part of this is due to a cultural shift since the 1950s. As with bowling leagues, women's social groups, and political parties, people aren't joining organizations as they used to. The 50s were a high-water mark for church attendance. But we are no longer a "joining" culture. Economic and social forces propelled women into the workplace; many are working more, with less leisure time—and how that leisure time is spent is not always in church. Now that the old "blue laws" have fallen into disuse, one can shop on Sunday or attend a school-sponsored sports event.

However, this is not to say that churches are blameless. Churches are not unlike restaurants: people will stand in line when they find a good one. It is incumbent upon us to do the kinds of things and be the kind of people that have made Christianity such an important part of our lives. Americans are hungry for meaning, purpose, and adventure. These are all integral to living the Christian life. The church has myriad amazing possibilities before it, and its mission is its charge from God: to worship and to study God's will, to work to help end hunger, combat racism, end war, and to stand up for human rights (just to name a few). The churches that are most deeply involved in focusing on God's will for themselves and for the world may be best equipped to encourage people to attend church on Sundays.

WHY (MOST) EPISCOPALIANS DON'T KICK DOGS

We don't advocate hitting kittens or starting forest fires, either.

In fact, caring for all of God's creation is something Episcopalians have long been interested in doing. As one of our prayers (BCP 388) puts it, "Give us all a reverence for the earth as your own creation, that we may use its resources rightly in the service of others and to your honor and glory." And as another (page 827) says,

> Almighty and everlasting God, you made the universe with all its marvelous order, its atoms, worlds, and galaxies, and the infinite complexity of living creatures: Grant that, as we probe the mysteries of your creation, we may come to know you more truly, and more surely fulfill our role in your eternal purpose; in the name of Jesus Christ our Lord. *Amen.*

This is why many Episcopal congregations sponsor an annual "Blessing of the Animals." It's often held in the fall, around the feast day of St. Francis of Assisi (October 4), famed for his love of his animal brothers and sisters. Some churches, like the Cathedral Church of St. John the Divine in New York, have welcomed horses, elephants, and camels into their sanctuary. Most others stick with dogs and cats, though iguanas, gerbils, and even snakes get in line. (Note to liturgical planners: keep the gerbils and snakes at opposite ends of the church.) The Episcopal Network for Animal Welfare (*enaw.org*), a sister organization to the Anglican Society for the Welfare of Animals, works to raise awareness of issues of animal cruelty and abuse.

Another grassroots organization working toward better stewardship of God's creation is the Episcopal Ecological Network (*eenonline.org*). This group advocates for the protection of the environment and preserving the sanctity of creation. When the heavens and the earth were created, God called it good—and we believe it still is. This is why we seek to not only care for it, as God has, but to bless it, as God continues to do.

WHY 70% OF EPISCOPALIANS WEREN'T BORN THAT WAY

Yes, we're a church of refugees.

It's no secret that the clear majority of those in Episcopal Church pews on Sunday mornings came from other Christian churches or from no church background at all. So, what's the draw?

Since so many come as adults, chances are that reason plays a role in a person's decision to become an Episcopalian. The Episcopal Church has consistently been labeled a "middle road"—a *"via media"*—between Roman Catholicism and Protestantism. We cultivate the reverence and rootedness of an ancient tradition alongside a clear devotion to the Bible. Although we have ordained ministers (including the bishops that give us our name), we also value the shared ministry of all believers. In years past, in fact, some people suggested that were America to unite under one national church, it just might be the Episcopal Church. It's worth noting that the National Cathedral in Washington, DC, host to some of the nation's most important religious events, is an Episcopal church.

Other people become Episcopalians because of our views on Holy Communion, women's ordination, and human rights. Some love the music, others the worship styles. Some marry into the church. And some come because it's convenient (there are about 7,000 Episcopal congregations in the United States, Europe, the Caribbean, Central and South America, and the Pacific).

Speaking of international issues, it is important to note that the Episcopal Church is a constituent member of the Anglican Communion—about which you can find more on pages 195 and 199. Many people who are now Episcopalians were formerly members of other churches in this Anglican family, and became part of the Episcopal Church when they emigrated.

No matter why people come, we like to think that we are a place of welcome. Wherever people are on their spiritual journey, our parishes strive to receive them with joy, understanding, and warmth. We don't pressure people or force them to believe. Rather, our congregations tend to thrive by providing an atmosphere of open curiosity, allowing people to ask and answer questions. We strive to let the Holy Spirit work. And when we do this, we find many people choosing the Episcopal Church.

WHY THE EPISCOPAL CHURCH IS (AND ISN'T) CATHOLIC LITE

It's both a catchy joke and an apt description—Catholic Lite.

The late comedian Robin Williams (an Episcopalian) popularized this term in an interview when, referring to a beer commercial, he described the Episcopal Church as "Catholic Lite . . . same rituals, half the guilt." As with many jokes, there's a nugget of truth in there, and one in which Episcopalians take some pride.

The Episcopal Church is a descendant of the Church of England, which was itself founded in 597 as a mission outpost of the Roman Catholic Church, through St. Augustine of Canterbury at the direction of Pope St. Gregory the Great. A variety of factors led to the parting of the ways between England and Rome some 500 years ago, and it's one that we're still working to heal. But we are indebted to and appreciative of the many rituals, traditions, and ways of believing in Christ that came to us through the Roman Catholic strand of our heritage.

And as is true of the Roman Catholic Church, the Episcopal Church has changed and evolved. The two churches have come down on the same side of many issues, but on different sides of others. We are perceived as being less strict, allowing priests to marry and non-Episcopalians to receive Holy Communion, and publicly allowing a wider breadth of acceptable belief and practice than one might find in a Roman Catholic Church. It is not that we don't have core beliefs, but that the things we consider core beliefs are fewer in number.

However, the impression that being an Episcopalian lacks rigor and demand is the downside to Williams' description; and the saying, "Episcopalians can believe anything they want" is just as inaccurate as saying, "We're just like Rome without the pope." There is nothing "lite" about being a Christian, no matter the church of which one is a member. Episcopalians promise in their baptismal vows to pray, take communion, to work for justice and peace and to respect the dignity of every human being, and to spread the Gospel, and that is a high responsibility.

DO EPISCOPALIANS BELIEVE IN CONFIRMATION?

Sure.

However, like many Christians, we have our own take on it. Episcopalians believe confirmation is an important step in the spiritual development of all believers, especially those baptized at an early age. In this case, it is expected that when one is ready and has been prepared, a mature public affirmation of faith be made. This involves a pledge to recommit to the responsibilities in the Baptismal Covenant, made in the presence of a bishop.

Some parishes recommend a particular age, usually between 13 and 16, while others wait until a young person expresses interest. Much depends on the "maturity" of the individual. (Some 14 year olds are more mature than some in their 20s!)

While confirmation used to be thought of as a "completion of baptism" and a requirement for receiving Holy Communion, this is no longer the case. Baptism is now better understood as complete initiation as a member of the church, and all the baptized are welcome to receive Holy Communion.

Confirmation includes the laying on of hands by a bishop. When the bishop does this, the bishop also prays for the candidate's continued growth in the Christian life and ministry, under the guidance of the Holy Spirit.

So confirmation is all about gearing up and energizing the spiritual life of any Christian. This is why members may also undergo this rite even if already confirmed in the Episcopal Church or another church, being received or reaffirming their baptismal vows in the bishop's presence, again with the laying on of episcopal hands with prayer. Sometimes a fire needs to be fanned a bit to rekindle.

DO EPISCOPALIANS BELIEVE IN THE CREEDS?

Believe in them? We even memorize them!

As with most churches, Episcopalians have a high regard for the historic creeds of the Christian faith. You will find the Nicene Creed included in the main Sunday liturgies at nearly every Episcopal church. The Apostles' Creed is found in the daily offices of Morning and Evening Prayer in the Book of Common Prayer, and it is recited in dialogue form as an affirmation of faith at baptism and confirmation, and at the Renewal of Baptismal Vows.

These creeds are more than 1,500 years old and are regarded as embodying the essential core of the Christian faith. They describe our understanding of God the Father, Son, and Holy Spirit, as well as the place and role of the church. When we recite them on Sundays we realize we are not only confirming our unity with millions of other Christians around the world, but with millions more who have preceded us in a common faith.

Also included in the BCP is the Creed of Saint Athanasius, which is found toward the back in a section labeled "Historical Documents" (page 864). This is not normally recited at worship, but is included as one of the traditional writings that have shaped the Episcopal Church. (It is also the source of one of the best witticisms of the English church tradition: "Our vicar is like God; invisible on weekdays and incomprehensible on Sundays.")

The creeds play an important role in the ongoing formation of the Episcopal Church. We continue to rely on their principles as "a sufficient statement of the Christian faith" (BCP 877) as we take our faith into the new millennium. Having a firm foundation is the best assurance for forward movement.

DO EPISCOPALIANS GO TO CONFESSION?

There is an old saying concerning the sacramental rites of the church—including the Reconciliation of a Penitent, or Confession—*all may, none must, and some should.*

This is a popular way of describing what many Episcopalians believe about this rite.

Episcopalians believe that sometimes a personal act of penitence and confession to another individual is the best way to deal with a burdened conscience. But it is not required of anyone. We have a liturgy for it in the Book of Common Prayer (page 447). It is open to all who feel the need to express their penitence in this way, taking 1 John 1:9 literally: "If we confess our sins, he who is faithful and just will forgive us our sins and cleanse us from all unrighteousness."

People most often take advantage of this rite in the spring, during Holy Week. A priest commonly serves as the confessor, as priests and bishops are permitted to pronounce absolution. However, Episcopalians also believe any Christian can hear a confession and use the provided declaration of forgiveness instead of absolution.

This rite is carried out in privacy, often in a worship area, with the confessor sitting behind the altar rail and the penitent kneeling, although face-to-face reconciliation in church pews or in a space set aside for that purpose is increasingly popular. After the confession is heard, the confessor may give counsel and encouragement, and even assign a psalm, prayer, or something to be done as a sign of penitence and as an act of thanksgiving.

The content of all confessions are not a matter of subsequent conversation. Confidentiality is morally absolute for the confessor and may not, under any circumstances, be broken.

HOW EPISCOPALIANS USE THREE-LEGGED STOOLS

Just like dairy farmers.

Of course, Episcopalians use three-legged stools to sit firmly and securely while we go about our work. However, we also use the three-legged stool as a metaphor for the way we define sources of authority in the Episcopal Church.

The three legs of this stool are Scripture, Tradition, and Reason. Holy Scripture is paramount and governing for matters of salvation, as a way of defining core beliefs. Does that mean we take the Bible literally? We begin with the "letter" (which is what "literal" means) but often dig deeper for the meaning, because we take the Bible seriously.

When Episcopalians talk about Tradition, we are referring to the many ways that the saints before us have dealt with issues of faith and doctrine. Let's face it, there are many modern concerns upon which Scripture is silent, like nuclear warfare, so we consult the thoughts and writings of ancestors in the faith to help us make a way forward.

The third leg is Reason—a necessary tool in understanding both the Scripture and the tradition. Reason involves both common sense and the wisdom to draw on the very broadest scope of human understanding, along with the deep well of personal experience. Of course, Reason is far from perfect, and it cannot on its own bring us to faith. There are some truths that cannot be proved, but only believed, and among these are the truths about God revealed by Scripture, which Reason can understand, but not demonstrate or prove. Still, one of God's greatest gifts is that part of the human that rests between our shoulders. In fact, speaking of Tradition, it is the *rational mind* that is traditionally designated as the residence of the Divine Image in human beings.

So when it comes to defining faith and doctrine, we use all three legs grounded and balanced, so that the whole enterprise won't topple over. Whether we are talking about matters of religion, or milking a cow, keeping a balanced stability is of great importance.

WHY ARE EPISCOPALIANS SO WISHY-WASHY?

Some have described the Episcopal Church as "the bland leading the bland."

For centuries Episcopalians have had a milquetoast reputation. We're not comfortable being in the spotlight, we're often willing to listen to both sides of an argument, and live-and-let-live big-tent thinking sits well with the vast majority of us. Some people criticize us for being unwilling to take a stand. Others compliment us for our even-handedness. So why do Episcopalians luxuriate in the lackluster?

It is helpful to keep that big tent in mind. It isn't so much about reaching a compromise that everybody can live with but that satisfies nobody; it's about having a comprehensive space in which sometimes contradictory beliefs can be accommodated together. It isn't about being wishy-washy in one's own mind, but respecting the minds of others, agreeing to disagree.

The penchant we have for *comprehension* (rather than compromise) comes to us quite naturally. As spiritual progeny of the Church of England, Episcopalians have inherited an English proclivity toward finding broad ground on which those on two extremes can both keep at least one foot. It's called the *via media*, the *middle way*. Formed amidst the battles between Roman Catholics and Protestants in the fifteenth century, the Church of England embraced and promoted comprehension as a way to stop the quarreling (and killing) and get on with the work of proclaiming the Gospel of Jesus Christ.

On a practical level we all know that you can be assured that the truth is present by having every reasonable option available. That's why most Episcopal churches are known for their openness and willingness to listen. Years ago we promoted ourselves as a place where "you don't need to check your brains at the door," where open and honest dialogue is welcomed. This sense of balance may be one reason for this fact: more U.S. Supreme Court justices have been from the Episcopal Church than any other.

A SHORT CHRONOLOGY OF THE EPISCOPAL CHURCH

597	St. Augustine arrives in Canterbury, sent by Pope St. Gregory the Great.
664	Synod of Whitby decides to favor Roman over Celtic traditions.
1534	Act of Supremacy gives the English monarch authority over the church.
1549	First Book of Common Prayer.
1558	Elizabeth I comes to English throne. Followed by "Elizabethan Settlement" that seeks to comprehend divided opinions.
1587	First Anglican worship and baptism in North Carolina.
1607	Founding of Jamestown colony in Virginia. Robert Hunt, priest, celebrates Holy Eucharist and leads daily Morning and Evening Prayer.
1624	Virginia becomes a royal colony, required to conform to Church of England (though without a bishop, confirmations, ordinations, etc.).
1640–60	Puritan rule in England.
1662	Restoration of English monarchy and Church of England; 1662 Book of Common Prayer issued (which will be the Prayer Book of the American colonial church).
1663	First church services in New York.
1701	Thomas Bray put in charge of church work in Maryland, founds Society for the Propagation of the Gospel, which sponsors over 300 missionaries in the colonies over the next century.

1738	John and Charles Wesley and George Whitefield, all Anglican priests, have religious experiences in Georgia. Evangelicalism gains popularity.
1776	Declaration of Independence by American colonies. Two-thirds of the signers are nominal members of the Church of England. Many Anglicans flee to Canada or remain as Tories.
1779	Charles Simeon, a scrupulous college student, becomes a priest and noted Anglican evangelical leader.
1784	Samuel Seabury consecrated first American bishop by Scottish bishops. A meeting in New York calls for a General Convention to ensure continuance of the church in the United States.
1785	First ordination in the United States (the Rev. Philo Shelton). First session of the General Convention. New Prayer Book proposed.
1787	Consecration of Bishops White and Provoost in London.
1789	General Convention adopts Constitution, Canons, and Book of Common Prayer.
1792	Bishop Thomas John Claggett of Maryland first Episcopal Bishop consecrated in the United States.
1794	St. Thomas' African Episcopal Church admitted to the Diocese of Pennsylvania.
1804	Absalom Jones, the Episcopal Church's first African-American priest, ordained.
1821	Founding of the General Theological Seminary.
1833	John Keble, Edward Pusey, and John Henry Newman found the Oxford Movement, a revival of catholic principles in worship and doctrine.
1835	Founding of the Domestic and Foreign Missionary Society. Jackson Kemper ordained first missionary bishop to American frontier. Missions to China and Africa begin.

1859   *Hymnal* revision begins.

1861–65 Founding of the Protestant Episcopal Church of the Confederate States of America and its seamless reunion with the Episcopal Church at war's end.

1871   Order of deaconesses revived (formally recognized in 1889).

1874   James Holly the first African-American bishop, ordained for ministry in Haiti.

1886   Quadrilateral on church unity adopted by House of Bishops. Ratified by Lambeth Conference 1888. Adopted by House of Deputies in 1892. William Reed Huntington, priest, is author.

1889   United Thank Offering is founded.

1892   Revised Book of Common Prayer and *Hymnal* adopted.

1917   Edward Thomas Demby (Arkansas) and Henry Beard Delaney (North Carolina) elected suffragan bishops, the first African-American bishops for domestic ministry.

1918   Publication of the *Hymnal* leads to formation of what is now the Church Pension Group.

1919   The National Council of the Episcopal Church (later renamed the Executive Council) established.

1928   Revised Book of Common Prayer adopted.

1940   Revision of *Hymnal*.

1944   Henry St. George Tucker becomes first Presiding Bishop required to resign his previous jurisdiction as diocesan.

1948   World Council of Churches convenes in Amsterdam as a "fellowship of churches which confess Jesus Christ as God and Savior." Archbishop of Canterbury Geoffrey Fisher presides.

1967   General Convention establishes Special Program to address issues of race and poverty.

1969	John Burgess elected bishop of Massachusetts, the first African-American diocesan bishop.
1970	General Convention approves change in Constitution to allow women to serve as Deputies, and the ordination of women as deacons.
1971	Harold Stephen Jones, first Native-American bishop, elected Suffragan of South Dakota.
1974	Eleven women ordained as priests in Philadelphia, Pennsylvania.
1976	Episcopal Church General Convention approves ordination of women to all three orders: bishop, priest, and deacon. Approval of major Draft Revision of Book of Common Prayer. Declaration that "homosexual persons are children of God who have a full and equal claim . . . upon the love, acceptance, and pastoral concern and care of the Church."
1979	Revised Book of Common Prayer adopted. *Hymnal* revision continues.
1982	Revision of *Hymnal* adopted.
1989	Barbara Harris consecrated bishop suffragan of Massachusetts: first woman bishop in the Anglican Communion.
1991	Stephen Charleston elected first Native-American diocesan bishop (Alaska).
1996	Bishop Walter Righter tried for heresy for having ordained an openly partnered gay man, Barry Stopfel, in 1990; Trial Court rules that there was no violation of "core doctrine."
2000	General Convention recognizes (resolution D039) that there are same-sex couples in life-long committed relationships which it expects to be "characterized by fidelity, monogamy, mutual affection and respect,

careful, honest communication, the holy love which enables those in such relationships to see in each other the image of God."

2003   Gene Robinson, an openly gay priest, consecrated as bishop of New Hampshire.

2006   Katharine Jefferts Schori elected and consecrated first female Presiding Bishop of the Episcopal Church and first female primate in the Anglican Communion.

2012   General Convention approves provisional rite for blessing of same-sex partnerships (*I Will Bless You and You Will Be a Blessing*, available with resources in an expanded format from Church Publishing Incorporated); forms Task Force for the Study of Marriage, and a Task Force on Restructuring to look at ways to adapt the church to changing circumstances.

FIVE EPISCOPALIANS WHO SHAPED THE CHURCH

Samuel Seabury

He was our first bishop. The Church of England declined to post a bishop in the American colonies, necessitating a long journey back to England every time someone was to be confirmed or ordained. Following the Revolutionary War, Seabury, who hailed from Connecticut, traveled to England in 1783. Since he could no longer take an oath of allegiance to the king, Seabury went to Scotland to be consecrated, and through that enriched the American Episcopal liturgy, since Scottish Episcopalians had retained texts deleted in English revisions. He returned to America and put his gifts to work, collaborating in laying a firm foundation for the Episcopal Church.

John Jay

He was a long-lived Episcopal lay leader, as well as a major figure in the American Revolution and the emergence of the United States. He was a contributor to the *Federalist Papers,* President of the Continental Congress, and served on numerous diplomatic missions and as the first Chief Justice of the Supreme Court. As a deputy to the first General Conventions, he influenced the development of the church's political structure in a way that won the approval of the Church of England, and personally paved the way for the consecration of Bishops White and Provoost. He was a charter member of the Domestic and Foreign Missionary Society, an early opponent of slavery, and a founder of the American Bible Society.

William White

Since it takes three bishops to consecrate a bishop, no sooner had Samuel Seabury returned from Scotland than the young American church put forward another candidate for bishop, William White of Philadelphia. By the time he arrived in England in 1787, the atmosphere had become more welcoming toward Americans, in part through John Jay's efforts, so he and Samuel Provoost of New York were consecrated as our second and third bishops. White was a devout pastor, founding several charitable and educational institutions to help the poor, the deaf, and a ministry devoted to helping prostitutes rebuild their lives. White also served as the Episcopal Church's first Presiding Bishop. His *Memoirs of the Protestant Episcopal Church* (the 1836 second edition is available free online in ebook format) provide a fascinating glimpse into the formative years of the church, from his unique perspective.

Julia Chester Emery

Emery served as the National Secretary for the Woman's Auxiliary of the Board of Missions of the Episcopal Church for forty years (1876–1916), during which time she visited every jurisdiction in the United States. In 1908, she attended the Pan-Anglican Congress and Lambeth Conference. She also traveled to mission outposts in China, Japan, and the Philippines, encouraging the work there, especially the mission work of women, as well as educational efforts. She encouraged the revival of the order of deaconess, and was a moving force in the creation of the United Thank Offering (UTO), a testament to the power of united efforts in giving for mission work around the world.

William Reed Huntington

He gained the nickname "First Presbyter of the Episcopal Church" because while elected bishop several times, he always declined to accept, as he preferred to remain a parish priest in the two parishes he served: All Saints, Worcester, Massachusetts (1862–1883) and Grace, Manhattan (1883–1909). In 1870 he wrote *The Church Idea,* in which he described the nucleus of what would later become the Chicago-Lambeth Quadrilateral, as the essential basis for church unity. Built upon the four foundations of Scripture, Sacraments (Baptism and Eucharist), Creeds, and Episcopate, this Quadrilateral has guided the development of the Anglican Communion in its ecumenical relationships with churches from other Christian traditions.

FIVE INSPIRING
BLACK EPISCOPALIANS

Absalom Jones

Born a slave in Delaware in 1746, Absalom Jones went on to become one whom many believe was the first black American to receive formal ordination in any denomination. A contemporary of Richard Allen, founder of the African Methodist Episcopal Church (AME Zion), Jones was also a well-known Philadelphia abolitionist and orator, preaching often (and memorably) against slavery. Jones petitioned Congress regarding the 1793 Fugitive Slave Act, lobbying for leniency and better treatment for blacks. He was the founder of the African Episcopal Church of St. Thomas, which continues as a vibrant congregation. The Episcopal Church honors his life each February 13.

Thurgood Marshall

He has been called the most important African-American Episcopalian of the twentieth century. Marshall was the first African-American to serve on the United States Supreme Court. As an attorney, he crisscrossed the South, filing civil rights lawsuits on behalf of the NAACP. He argued and won 29 of 32 cases before the Supreme Court. Marshall may be best remembered for winning the 1954 *Brown vs. Board of Education* case, which declared segregation in public schools unconstitutional. Marshall served on the vestry at St. Philip's in Harlem, and later worshiped at St. Augustine's in southwest Washington, DC, where a community center bears his name.

John Burgess

Burgess served as bishop in the Episcopal Diocese of Massachusetts for 13 years, first as bishop suffragan from 1962 to 1969. He was elected as bishop coadjutor in 1969 and served as diocesan bishop from 1970 to 1975—thus becoming the first African-American to head a diocese in the Episcopal Church. While serving as Episcopal chaplain at Howard University in Washington, DC, Burgess was also named a canon at Washington National Cathedral. His preaching there in the 1950s roused the social conscience of the Episcopal Church and nurtured the seeds of the church's involvement in the civil rights movement. Burgess was known for his commitment to the welfare of the urban poor and for his desire that the Church be a force for social change beyond its doors. "I just wanted to prove that the Episcopal Church could be relevant to the lives of the poor," he said in a 1992 interview.

Colin Powell

The son of Jamaican immigrants, Gen. Colin Luther Powell was raised in New York's South Bronx, where he served as an acolyte at St. Margaret's Episcopal Church. He calls the Episcopal Church a pillar of his life, and says it helped instill the discipline, structure, camaraderie, and the sense of belonging that became very important to him as his career took off. At age 49, he became President Ronald Reagan's National Security Advisor. At 52, he became the youngest person—and first African-American—to serve as Chairman of the Joint Chiefs of Staff. In 2001, under President George W. Bush, he became the first African-American U.S. Secretary of State.

Carol Moseley Braun

An attorney and political leader, Moseley Braun is the first woman from Illinois and the first African-American woman to be elected to the United States Senate. She grew up and studied in Chicago, eventually earning her law degree from the University of Chicago in 1974. This led to a long career in law and politics. Although she was raised as a Roman Catholic, in 1986 a raft of troubles in her personal and political life produced a crisis of faith and she had an experience of being born again. She is a member of St. Paul the Redeemer Episcopal Church.

FIVE INSPIRING WOMEN EPISCOPALIANS

Eleanor Roosevelt

One of the most admired women of the twentieth century, she was First Lady of the United States from 1933–1945. Known as a reformer, diplomat, and humanitarian, she was a cradle Episcopalian, making her church home at St. James' in Hyde Park, New York. Along with raising five children and supporting her husband, Franklin Delano Roosevelt, she was an outspoken advocate of equal rights, child welfare, and labor reforms. She served as the U.S. delegate to the United Nations and played a key role in the adoption of the Universal Declaration of Human Rights in 1948.

Sandra Day O'Connor

This esteemed jurist was the first woman to serve on the United States Supreme Court. Appointed by President Ronald Reagan in 1981, Justice O'Connor served the high court for 24 years before retiring. During this time she was consistently voted one of America's most powerful women. Her gender restricted opportunities to work as an attorney following graduation from Stanford University's law school, so she turned to public service in California, then Germany, then in her home state of Arizona. She was elected judge in Maricopa County in 1975. Her professionalism and fairness made her one of the most respected justices in recent memory.

Pamela Pauly Chinnis

Chinnis was the first woman elected President of the Episcopal Church's House of Deputies. She was elected in 1991, and re-elected in 1994 and 1997, for three three-year terms. Her presidency, coming only 21 years after the first woman deputy was granted seat, voice, and vote in the House, marked a major milestone in the leadership of lay women in the highest levels of Episcopal Church governance. She was a staunch supporter of the role of the House of Deputies, repeatedly reminding its members that it was the "senior" house (having existed prior to there being any bishops) and that "Laity, clergy and bishops have an equal voice in determining policy, establishing our legal framework, and maintaining a living liturgical life." In her hometown of Washington, DC, she worshiped and served in numerous leadership roles at Church of the Epiphany and served on the cathedral chapter of Washington National Cathedral.

Barbara Harris

The first woman to be consecrated bishop not only in the Episcopal Church, but in the Anglican Communion, Harris came to ministry as former head of public relations for the Sun Oil Company. Long active in civil rights campaigns, she participated in freedom rides and marches in the South in the 1960s. After discerning a call to ministry, she was ordained priest in 1980. She served as publisher and later board member of the Episcopal Church Publishing Company's progressive magazine, *The Witness*. She was consecrated as a bishop suffragan in 1989 in the Diocese of Massachusetts, where she served for 13 years until her retirement.

Katharine Jefferts Schori

She is the first woman Presiding Bishop of the Episcopal Church and the first female primate in the Anglican Communion. Since 2006 her leadership has emphasized advocacy for the poor and marginalized. She is a strong proponent of the United Nations' Millennium Development Goals and an outspoken advocate on environmental issues. During her time in office, Jefferts Schori has been challenged in keeping both conservative and liberal elements of the church together. She has a background in biology and oceanography, and is a licensed pilot. As bishop of Nevada, she piloted her plane around the diocese for visitations.

FIVE FAMOUS
EPISCOPALIAN WRITERS

John Steinbeck

Instantly recognized by many a high school literature student, Steinbeck is probably best known for his works of Depression-era fiction, *The Grapes of Wrath* (1939) and *Of Mice and Men* (1937). Steinbeck won the Pulitzer Prize and the Nobel Prize for literature, and published a total of 25 books. Steinbeck was born and raised in Salinas, California. He served as an acolyte and choir member at St. Paul's Episcopal Church in Salinas where, it is said, he dropped a cross onto a visiting bishop's head and thus lost his lead acolyte privileges. Many of Steinbeck's books were also made into plays and films, including *Tortilla Flat* (1942), *The Red Pony* (1949), and *East of Eden* (1955).

Madeleine L'Engle

A prolific writer of young adult fiction, L'Engle is probably best known for her Newbery Medal-winning novel, *A Wrinkle in Time* (1962) and its sequels, A *Wind in the Door* (1973), *A Swiftly Tilting Planet* (1978), *Many Waters* (1986), and *An Acceptable Time* (1989). L'Engle's writings exhibit a strong interest in modern science as well as religion. She became volunteer librarian at the Cathedral of St. John the Divine in New York City in 1965. Later she was named writer-in-residence there. L'Engle's belief in the breadth of salvation informed her stories. She was criticized by some Christians as liberal and at the same time by secular critics for being too religious.

William Faulkner

One of the most influential authors of the twentieth century, Faulkner was a prolific writer of novels and short stories. He won two Pulitzer Prizes and the Nobel Prize. His most popular works include *The Sound and the Fury* (1929), *As I Lay Dying* (1930), *Light in August* (1932), *Absalom, Absalom!* (1936), and "A Rose for Emily" (1932). Most of his stories were based in his native Mississippi, where he attended St. Peter's Episcopal Church in Oxford. Faulkner was known for his "Southern Gothic" stream-of-consciousness writing style. Though not an outwardly religious man, his gifts of creativity and intelligence earned him an unparalleled place in American literary history.

Wystan Hugh Auden

W.H. Auden was born in England but became an American citizen and an Episcopalian. He wrote many essays but is best known for his poetry and his opera libretti (including collaborations with Benjamin Britten and Igor Stravinsky). Well established among a handful of others as one of the great poets of the twentieth century, he gained a posthumous bump in his reputation when one of his poems was recited in the movie *Four Weddings and a Funeral.* He was a great lover of language, and served as a consultant on the translation of the Psalms for the 1979 Book of Common Prayer. A staunch opponent of what he saw as "dumbed-down" language, he helped preserve the cadences of the Coverdale translation of the Psalms that had formed a part of the BCP since 1549. A section of one of his poems, "For the Time Being," has two settings in *The Hymnal 1982.*

Tennessee Williams

A legendary American playwright whose works won numerous awards, Thomas Lanier "Tennessee" Williams was the grandson of an Episcopal priest with whom he was particularly close. After suffering from a paralytic disease as a young boy, his mother gave him a typewriter. Williams would go on to write *The Glass Menagerie* (1945), *A Streetcar Named Desire* (1948), *The Rose Tattoo* (1952), and *Cat on a Hot Tin Roof* (1965). Later in life he attended Roman Catholic churches. His literary rights now belong to Sewanee, The University of the South, which uses the funds to support a creative writing program.

FIVE FAMOUS PERFORMING EPISCOPALIANS (OK, TEN)

In order of appearance

Edward Kennedy "Duke" Ellington

You can't do justice to the history of music in the twentieth century without acknowledging the influence of composer and musician Duke Ellington. Although well known as a performer and conductor, his most lasting legacy is as a composer, included by Percy Grainger in the ranks of Bach and Delius. His score for *Anatomy of a Murder* (in which he also appears) was the first by an African-American composer in which the music is not performed by on-screen musicians, as in many of his earlier films, where he is seen leading his orchestra. In the 1960s he composed and performed the *Sacred Concerts,* which he described as "the most important work I've done." He continued composing until shortly before his death in 1974. Over 12,000 attended his funeral at the Cathedral Church of St. John the Divine in New York City.

Fred Astaire

Many believe him to be the most talented dancer of the twentieth century. Fred Astaire was an Oscar-winning film star and Broadway stage dancer, choreographer, singer, and actor. He paired with Ginger Rogers in ten films, including *Top Hat* (1935), *Swing Time* (1936), and *Shall We Dance* (1937). He was a talented though modest singer who also co-wrote (with Johnny Mercer) the top-ten hit, "I'm Building Up to an Awful Letdown" (1936). While not yet a teenager, the young Astaire met an Episcopal priest in New York City and was confirmed at the Church of the Transfiguration, which became home to the Episcopal Actors' Guild. During his life he is said to have enjoyed the quiet and calming atmosphere of St. Bartholomew's in New York City as well as All Saints' in Beverly Hills, California, where he spent long hours of contemplation.

Judy Garland

One of Hollywood's most acclaimed entertainers, Judy Garland's versatility garnered her many awards, though she lived a difficult life. She won an Academy Award, a Golden Globe, Grammy awards, and a Tony. She is perhaps best known as Dorothy from *The Wizard of Oz* (1939) and for her memorable rendition of "Somewhere Over the Rainbow." Born Frances Ethel Gumm in Grand Rapids, Michigan, she was baptized at the local Episcopal parish where her father, a vaudeville performer, served as choral director. Garland starred in dozens of productions, including *Meet Me in St. Louis* (1944), *Easter Parade* (1948), and *A Star Is Born* (1954). Married five times, Garland endured a decades-long struggle with addiction before her death at age 47. Her legacy includes daughter Liza Minnelli and a ranking among the American Film Institute's top ten greatest female stars in the history of American cinema.

Judy Collins

Known for her distinctive soprano voice and her wide repertoire, Grammy winner Judy Collins came of age during the 1960s folk revival, singing songs by Bob Dylan and Pete Seeger. Her piercing eyes were the inspiration for Crosby, Stills, and Nash's hit song, "Suite: Judy Blue Eyes." Her versions of "Amazing Grace" and "Send in the Clowns" were top 20 hits. Collins' version of Joni Mitchell's "Chelsea Morning" inspired Bill and Hillary Clinton in naming their daughter. Raised in the United Methodist Church, Collins married husband Louis Nelson at the Cathedral of St. John the Divine in New York City, where to this day she often goes to pray and to sing. "I think of Jesus as a total rebel because he was saying things that were completely out—forgive your enemies? Are you kidding? What a concept. Very revolutionary, actually."

Sam Waterston

An Academy Award-nominated actor, Sam Waterston is probably best known for his role on the long-running television series *Law and Order*. Waterston began playing the role of D.A. Jack McCoy in 1994. Nominated for a Best Actor Academy Award in 1985 for *The Killing Fields,* Waterston has won a Primetime Emmy, a Golden Globe, and a Screen Actors Guild award. Though known for crusty characters such as Charlie Skinner in HBO's *The Newsroom,* Waterston is also a classically trained theater actor, who has extensive credits performing Shakespeare and other classics. Other credits include *The Great Gatsby* (1974) and *Crimes and Misdemeanors* (1989). An active humanitarian and Episcopalian, Waterston has aided Refugees International, Meals on Wheels, the United Way, and the Episcopal Actors' Guild, and has led fundraising activities for the General Theological Seminary and Episcopal Charities in New York.

Bobby McFerrin

Although Manhattan-born McFerrin is perhaps best known for his 1988 Grammy Award winning hit song, "Don't Worry, Be Happy," and for his incredibly versatile singing style—which often gives the impression of polyphony—he has also guest-conducted many of the world's great symphony orchestras and written sacred music. This includes his moving adaptation and setting of the 23rd Psalm, dedicated to his mother, as a meditative Anglican chant. In 2009, he joined Daniel Levitin as co-host of an award-winning PBS documentary *The Music Instinct.* He is committed to the notion of music as "medicine for the soul."

Robin Williams

Williams, who died on August 11, 2014, was among the most popular comedians of the twentieth century. He won numerous awards, including an Oscar, six Golden Globes, and a Screen Actors Guild award. His film credits include *Good Morning Vietnam* (1987), *Dead Poets Society* (1989), *Mrs. Doubtfire* (1993), and *Good Will Hunting* (1997). He was best known for his extraordinary improvisational skills and spot-on impersonations. Williams was voted thirteenth on *Comedy Central Presents: 100 Greatest Stand-Ups of All Time.* Raised in a parish in suburban Detroit, Williams was never timid about making fun of his WASP roots. "I'm an Episcopalian," he once said. "It's Catholic Lite—same rituals, half the guilt." Williams also came up with the oft-quoted "Top Ten Reasons to Be an Episcopalian." He was active in many charity and outreach efforts, including fundraising to rebuild the cathedral in Christchurch, New Zealand.

Rosanne Cash

Often classified as a country musician, largely because of the success of her father, Johnny Cash, Rosanne Cash's music includes pop, rock, and folk influences. Cash joined her father's traveling show when she graduated from high school and gradually worked her way up to singing back-up vocals. After finally going out on her own, she had several country hits including "Seven Year Ache" (1981), "It's Such a Small World" (with Rodney Crowell, 1988), and "Runaway Train" (1988). Although her mother was a strict Roman Catholic and her father was a Baptist, Cash felt they were open to allowing her to undertake her own spiritual journey, which includes attending Episcopal liturgies. "I consider myself religious in the best sense of the word . . . I pray every single day and I meditate every single day. So my spiritual life is as important to me as my creative life."

David Hyde Pierce

He is best known for his performances on the long-running hit television sitcom *Frazier.* Pierce spent 11 years on the program in the role of Dr. Niles Crane, for which he won four Emmy Awards. His film credits include *Little Man Tate* (1991), *Sleepless in Seattle* (1993), and *Down with Love* (2003). Pierce is also a talented stage performer and singer, winning a Tony Award in 2007 for his performance in the Broadway musical *Curtains.* In 2012–13 he appeared off and on Broadway in Christopher Durang's Tony Award-winning play, *Vanya and Sonia and Masha and Spike.* Growing up in Saratoga Springs, New York, Pierce spent time on the organ bench at his parish, Bethesda Episcopal Church, which is known for its outstanding music program. Pierce is an active supporter of Alzheimer's research, AIDS charities, and lesbian, gay, bisexual, and transgender causes.

Courtney Cox

She's probably best known as one of the lead characters in the popular long-running sitcom *Friends*. Courtney Cox began her public career as a model, then appeared in a Bruce Springsteen video ("Dancing in the Dark") and a few supporting television roles before landing a lead role in the ensemble cast of *Friends*. She married her former husband, actor David Arquette, at Grace Cathedral in San Francisco during her ten-year run on the sitcom. A few years later they returned to her hometown of Birmingham, Alabama, where their first child, Coco Riley, was baptized at St. Stephen's Episcopal Church. Actress Jennifer Aniston is the child's godmother.

TEN FAMOUS HYMNS
WRITTEN BY EPISCOPALIANS

Episcopalian poets and composers have made considerable contributions to Christian hymnody. Here are some examples:

"I Sing a Song of the Saints of God"—music by John Henry Hopkins

"O Zion Haste, Thy Mission High Fulfilling"—words by Mary Ann Thomson

"Come with Us, O Blessed Jesus"—words by John Henry Hopkins, Jr.

"How Wondrous and Great Thy Works"—words by Henry Ustick Onderdonk

Episcopalians have done a good deal to enliven Christmastide and the Epiphany. What would either be like without these:

"Silent Night, Holy Night"—John Freeman Young translated the words of Joseph Mohr

"O Little Town of Bethlehem"—words by Phillips Brooks, music by Lewis H. Redner

"We Three Kings of Orient Are"—words and music by John Henry Hopkins, Jr.

And when it comes to our national musical heritage, how about these:

"O Say, Can You See?"—words by Francis Scott Key

"O Beautiful for Spacious Skies"—music by Samuel Augustus Ward

"God of Our Fathers" ("National Hymn")—words by Daniel Crane Roberts, music by George William Warren

FIVE FAMOUS SCIENTIFIC EPISCOPALIANS

Margaret Mead

A cultural anthropologist and well-known writer and speaker in the 1960s and 1970s, Margaret Mead may be best known for *Coming of Age in Samoa* (1928). Following graduate work at Columbia University, she spent many years working with the American Museum of Natural History in New York City. Her fieldwork in the South Pacific led her to report about the attitude toward sex in traditional cultures there. A devout Anglo-Catholic and regular churchgoer, she played a considerable role in drafting the 1979 Book of Common Prayer. Mead became a member of the Episcopal Church as an adult, and once said, "What I wanted was a form of religion that gave expression to an already existing faith." She was awarded the Presidential Medal of Freedom posthumously.

Henry Field

Chicago-born anthropologist and archaeologist Henry Field was the great-nephew of the famous merchant Marshall Field. After studying in England, he came to work at the Field Museum of Natural History in his hometown. One of his major contributions was to oversee the creation of the "Hall of the Races of Mankind" for the opening of the 1933 World's Fair. He was tapped by Franklin D. Roosevelt as "Anthropologist to the President" and worked with him on top-secret plans for refugee resettlement that would soon become crucial. His 1934 expedition photographs of the Marsh Arabs of Iraq were featured in a 2004 exhibit at the Peabody Museum at Harvard.

Jeannette Piccard

A woman of many talents, Piccard was an accomplished scientist, teacher, priest, and aeronaut. A member of a family of balloonists, in 1934 she became the first pilot—and the first woman—to reach the stratosphere (57,579 feet). Piccard worked on several high-profile balloon projects alongside her husband, Jean Piccard. They are credited with the invention of the plastic balloon. Her life-long dream, however, was to become a priest. In 1974, at age 79, she made history as one of the Philadelphia 11—the first women to be ordained priests in the Episcopal Church, in a controversial liturgy preceding authorization of the ordination of women. Piccard served in Minnesota until her death at age 86.

Denton Cooley

Cooley is a heart surgeon who performed the first total artificial heart implant. He is the founder and chief surgeon at the Texas Heart Institute and St. Luke's Episcopal Hospital, Houston. His contributions to the field of cardiovascular medicine cannot be overestimated. In 1984 Ronald Reagan awarded him the Presidential Medal of Freedom, and in 1998 Bill Clinton presented him with the National Medal of Technology. Although renowned as a surgeon, in his own estimation he prizes his administrative work in developing the first "packaged pricing" plan for cardiovascular procedures—a proposal which helps to limit health care costs that has been widely adopted since.

Donald W. Douglas, Sr.

Douglas is the "D" in the name of the DC-10 airplane. He was an aeronautics pioneer and founder of the Douglas Company, which built the first airplane to lift a useful load exceeding its own weight. An outstanding student, Douglas graduated from Trinity Chapel School in New York City. He completed his four-year degree at MIT in two years and became an assistant professor in aeronautics there. After founding his own company in 1921, he secured military contracts and designed transport planes, finally launching one of the world's first commercial jetliners, the DC-8, in 1958. His company eventually merged with McDonnell Aircraft, then with Boeing. Douglas was not an outwardly religious man, though his innovative work helped millions of people soar above the heavens. Following his death, his ashes were scattered over the Pacific Ocean.

EPISCOPAL CHURCH SNAPSHOT

The Episcopal Church

- 6,700 congregations
- Average Sunday attendance at a "typical" parish—100 people
- 1.9 million active members
- 18,000 clergy (including retired)
- Total gross receipts over $2 billion per year
- 52 percent of churches built before 1950
- One of the 44 national and regional churches that make up the Anglican Communion (80 million members)
- Clergy are both men and women
- Clergy are called deacons, priests, and bishops (see the next page for exactly what to call them)
- *Episcopal* is an adjective, as in "the Episcopal Church." *Episcopalian* is a noun. A person is an Episcopalian, but does not attend an Episcopalian Church.

Note: A wealth of past and current statistical information concerning the Episcopal Church can be found at:

http://www.episcopalchurch.org/page/research-and-statistics.

WHAT DO YOU CALL THE CLERGY

Some might say, "Anything but late for supper!"

As with many things in the Episcopal Church, there is no specific rule, but there is a weight of tradition, and local custom varies. It is always fair to ask a priest how she or he wishes to be addressed. Many will simply ask that you use their Christian name.

There was a time when Anglo-Catholic or High Church priests were called "Father" while most others preferred "Mister." As the "Altitude Wars" have more or less subsided, many priests will now answer to "Father"—including a few priests who are women, though some of the latter prefer "Mother."

The one thing to which many Episcopal priests seem to be allergic is to be addressed as "Reverend," so that is best avoided.

When it comes to bishops and deacons, life is a bit easier, as it is customary and acceptable to say, "Hello, Bishop" or "Good morning, Deacon Jones." No one seems to know why saying "Good evening, Priest" has never caught on. But it hasn't; nor has "Presbyter." In some cases "Vicar" or "Rector" may be a welcome alternative, as appropriate and customary, but all in all this seems a matter of local style and tradition.

PROVINCES OF THE EPISCOPAL CHURCH

2013–2015 Triennium

Province II includes:
Convocation of Episcopal
Churches in Europe
Haiti
The Virgin Islands

PROVINCE V

PROVINCE II

PROVINCE I

Maine

Vermont

New Hampshire

Western Mass.

Massachusetts

Albany

Conn.

Rhode Island

Northern Michigan

Eau Claire

Fond du Lac

Eastern Michigan

Western New York

Central New York

Rochester

New York

Newark

Milwaukee

Western Michigan

Michigan

Long Island

Chicago

Northern Indiana

Ohio

N.W. Penn.

Central Pennsylvania

Bethlehem

Springfield

Indianapolis

Southern Ohio

Pittsburgh

Harrisburg

Maryland

Delaware

PROVINCE III

Missouri

West Virginia

Virginia

Easton

S.W. Virginia

S. Virginia

Washington

Lexington

Kentucky

North Carolina

West Tennessee

Tennessee

East Tennessee

Western N. Carolina

Upper S. Carolina

East Carolina

Alabama

Atlanta

The Episcopal Church in South Carolina

Mississippi

Georgia

Central Gulf Coast

Louisiana

Florida

PROVINCE IV

Central Florida

Southwest Florida

Southeast Florida

PROVINCE IX

Colombia,
Dominican Republic,
Ecuador Central,
Ecuador Litoral,
Honduras, Puerto Rico,
Venezuela

Under the Direction of the Presiding Bishop

Office of the Suffragan Bishop for Federal Ministries
(Hospitals, Prisons, Armed Forces)
The Episcopal Church in Micronesia
Convocation of Episcopal Churches in Europe

EVERYDAY STUFF

HOW TO CARE FOR THE SICK

Although reaching out to the sick is a ministry in which all can take part, it is good to remember that, as the Book of Common Prayer notes, "In case of illness, the Minister of the Congregation is to be notified" (page 453). Clergy are normally very glad to visit members of the church in the hospital or at home. This reflects the biblical advice in the Epistle of James (5:14): "Are any among you sick? They should call for the elders of the church and have them pray over them, anointing them with oil in the name of the Lord." Of course, it is always important to respect the wishes and privacy of any sick person, so it is good to ask someone if they would like the church to know of their condition before you notify the clergy.

Many parishes keep lists of those who are sick, hospitalized, or homebound, and include their names in public prayer. Again, it is important to ask if someone wishes their condition to be known, respecting their privacy. One can always pray privately.

While a trained and licensed physician must be sought to treat illness and injury, there is no malady that cannot be helped with faithful attention and prayer. Every Christian has the capacity to be a friend in need and offer prayerful kindness and support.

Be Aware

- Some people claim expertise in healing, but may have no training or accreditation. Use caution and skepticism, but keep an open mind.
- Many people believe that much healing can be found in "comfort foods," such as homemade chicken soup. The visit that accompanies the "hot dish" may be even more welcome and comforting.

- The ministry of listening is sometimes hard to practice. When a sick person is sharing their pain or illness with you, try not to respond with your own experiences, but rather with reaffirmation of their experience. Think, "That must feel terrible" rather than, "Oh, I had pains just like that." The ministry of comfort is not a competition.
- Those who attempt to diagnose and treat their own symptoms can often do more harm than good. Urge people with serious illness or conditions always to consult a doctor or other medical professional.

HOW TO CONSOLE A GRIEVING FRIEND

Consolation is a gift from God. Christians in turn give it to others to build up the body of Christ and preserve it in times of trouble. (See 2 Corinthians 1:4–7.) Episcopalians often employ food as a helpful secondary means.

Listen first.

Make it known that you're present and available. When the person opens up, be quiet and attentive. As with visiting the sick, this isn't about *you*.

Help the person face grief and sadness rather than avoiding them.

The object is to help them get in touch with their own feelings, and to identify, understand, and work through their feelings, not gloss over them.

Avoid saying things to make yourself feel better.

"I know exactly how you feel" is seldom true and trivializes the sufferer's pain. Even if you have experienced something similar, no experience is exactly the same. If there is nothing to say, simply be present with the person. A grammatical help is never to make yourself the subject of a sentence.

Show respect with honesty.

Don't try to answer the mysteries of the universe or force your beliefs on another. Be clear about the limitations of your abilities. Be ready to let some questions go unanswered. Consolation isn't about having answers, it's about bearing one another's burdens.

Don't put words in God's mouth.

Avoid such things as, "This is God's will," or, "This is part of God's plan." Unless you heard it straight from God, don't say it.

HOW TO COPE WITH LOSS AND GRIEF

Many people downplay their losses by saying, "Oh, I'm fine, thanks." This may provide temporary relief at best. Any loss can cause pain, feelings of confusion, and uncertainty. These responses are normal.

Become familiar with the stages of grief.

Experts identify five: denial, anger, bargaining, depression, and acceptance. Some add *hope* as a sixth stage. Grieving persons cycle back and forth through the stages, sometimes experiencing two or three in a single day. This is normal.

Express your grief.

Healthy expressions may include crying, staring into space for extended periods, ruminating, shouting at the ceiling, and sudden napping. Laughing outbursts are also common. The important thing is not to judge yourself. Own your feelings and let them be.

Identify someone you trust with whom to talk.

Available people can include a spouse, parents, relatives, friends, a doctor, or a trained counselor. And don't forget the clergy!

Choose a personal way to memorialize the loss.

Some of the greatest art has come from the greatest grief. Make a collage of photographs, start a scrapbook of memories to honor the event, write a poem or a story, or even a journal. This may help you begin to heal without getting stuck in grief. At some point, you may want to make a donation to your church for a physical memorial of some kind. This can be an act of closure and acceptance.

Be Aware

- A self-giving activity, such as volunteering at a shelter or soup kitchen, can be part of a healthy grieving process.
- The pain immediately after suffering a loss is usually sharp and intense. This may lessen with the passage of time, or fade to an ache. Allow yourself to "accompany" the pain. It will change or depart when you and it are ready.
- Anger, guilt, bitterness, and sadness are all emotions that may arise. Let them arise and pass over you and around you.
- Short-term depression may occur in some cases. There can also be physical effects brought on by grieving. After experiencing a great loss, such as the death of a loved one, make an appointment with your doctor to discuss both your feelings and your physical state.
- Even Jesus cried when his friend Lazarus died (John 11:35). There is no shame in grief.

HOW TO FORGIVE SOMEONE

Forgiving is one of the most difficult disciplines of faith, since it seems to cost you something additional when you've already been wronged. Swallowing your hurt and seeking a greater good, however, can yield great healing and growth.

Acknowledge that God forgives *you*.

When you realize that God has already shown forgiveness, and continues to forgive sinners like yourself, it is easier to forgive someone else. As Jesus said in the Lord's Prayer, the two are intimately related. Read Matthew 6:9–15.

Seek out the person who has offended you, if possible.

It may be best to extend your forgiveness in person. In cases where this is geographically impossible, find an appropriate alternative means, such as the telephone. One surprise that you might find is that the person isn't even aware of the offense, or may have been misunderstood.

Note: A face-to-face encounter may not always be the best way to forgive, given the timing of the situation or the level of hurt. Certain problems can be made worse by an unwelcome declaration of forgiveness. If you are in doubt, consider how you would feel if approached in a similar way.

Learn to say, "I forgive you," and mean it.

A verbal declaration of forgiveness is ideal. Speaking the words enacts a physical chain reaction that can create healing for both speaker and hearer. Throughout your conversation, using "I statements" is important (the opposite of when visiting the sick). For instance, instead of "You did . . . ," it is better to say, "I felt very hurt when. . . ." Owning your feelings is an important part of forgiving the hurt.

Pray for the power to forgive.

Praying for this is always good, whether a forgiveness situation is at hand or not. It is especially helpful in cases where declaring forgiveness seems beyond your reach. You might also like to review the beautiful "Prayer attributed to St. Francis" on page 833 of the Book of Common Prayer.

Be Aware

When someone sins against you personally, forgiving them does *not* depend upon *them* feeling sorry (showing contrition) or asking for your forgiveness. But it helps. You may have to struggle to forgive those who show no indication of responsibility for the action that injured you. Forgiveness can ease you of a burden even if the one forgiven doesn't feel responsible.

HOW TO PRAY

Prayer is intimate communication with God and can be used before a meal, at bedtime, during worship, or any time the need or opportunity arises. Silent and spoken prayers may be used liberally throughout the day. Prayer is also taking time to be open to God's prompting in our lives. Spontaneous prayer is often best, but the following process may help build the habit.

Assess your need for prayer.

Take stock of the situation at hand, including your motivations. What are you praying *for* and why?

Select a type of prayer.

There are many aspects to prayer. Prayers of *supplication* (requests for God's help), *contrition* (in which we confess sin and ask for forgiveness), *intercession* (prayer on behalf of others), *thanksgiving* (looking at the past and present and thanking God for blessings), and others are time-tested. One very widely popular sequence of prayer comes with the handy acronym A.C.T.S., moving through a sequence of Adoration, Confession, Thanksgiving, and ending with Supplication. In other words, take a moment to become aware of God's presence; ponder your faults and failings and acknowledge them to God; give thanks for blessings in your life; and then ask God for the help you seek—for yourself or others.

When it comes to specific prayers for particular intentions, the Book of Common Prayer, books of personal prayers, hymnals, and devotionals often contain helpful and thoughtful prayers already composed for particular needs.

Select a physical posture for prayer.

Many postures are appropriate:

- Kneeling with your face and palms upturned is good for prayers of supplication.

- Sitting comfortably with bowed head, closed eyes, and hands folded aids concentration.
- Consider that there are ways of "walking prayer." Many have found that walking in a pattern, such as that of the Prayer Labyrinth of Chartres Cathedral, helps them to focus their intentions.

There is no "official" posture for prayer. Choose your posture according to your individual prayer needs. If you are distracted by your posture, you will be thinking about it instead of your prayer.

Offer your prayer freely.

Pray with confidence and not under compulsion. Think of prayer as a gift, to you and to God. God hears all prayer and responds. Breathe deeply, relax, and be open as the Spirit leads you.

Listen.

Take time during your prayer simply to listen in silence. Some prayer traditions involve only silent meditation as a means of listening for God's voice. The "Jesus Prayer" of the Eastern Orthodox tradition is a form of "centering prayer" or "word prayer" in which one gently focuses on one's own breathing and a word or short phrase, to which one returns when distracted. One traditional phrase is adapted from the repeated appeal of the blind man Timaeus in Mark 10:47–48: "Jesus, Son of God, have mercy on me."

Be Aware

- As theologian Marjorie Hewitt Suchocki has noted, "Prayer is God's invitation to us to be willing partners in the great dance of bringing a world into being that reflects something of God's character." When we pray, we are on holy ground, and prayer reminds us where we are.
- Prayer can be made either alone or in the company of others (corporately). Most public worship includes the elements of A.C.T.S.

- Environment matters. If possible, consider lighting a candle and dimming the lights to set a quiet mood and help block out distractions.
- Making a habit of prayer may help you to find you can "pray always in the Spirit" (Ephesians 6:18).

HOW TO RESOLVE INTERPERSONAL CONFLICT

Disagreements are part of life. They often occur when we forget that not everyone sees things the same way. Conflict should be viewed as an opportunity to grow, not a contest for domination. Episcopalians can be rather reserved, but they value healthy—and healed—relationships.

Adopt a healthy attitude.

Your frame of mind is critical. Approach the situation with fore-thought and calm. Prayer can be invaluable at this stage. Do not approach the other party when you're angry or upset.

Read Matthew 18:15–20 and reflect on it.

This will orient your thinking. This is the model Jesus provided and can be used to call to mind an appropriate method.

Talk directly to the person with whom you disagree.

Avoid "triangulation." Talking about others to a third party can make the conflict worse, as they may rightly feel they are the sub-ject of gossip. Speaking with them directly eliminates the danger and boosts the odds of a good outcome.

Express yourself without attacking.

Using "I statements" can avoid casting the other person as the "bad guy" and inflaming the conflict. "I statements" are sentences beginning with phrases such as "I feel . . ." or "I'm uncomfort-able when. . . ."

Speak the truth in love (Ephesians 4:15).

Your perception may not be the other's. In fact, it really can't be, as all see through their own eyes. Sometimes disagreements arise from misunderstandings, so being clear about your own mind is crucial. Try not to blame others for misunderstanding you, and take responsibility when you have misunderstood others. Your objective is to discover and honor each other's experiences—which may be very different—not to put the other person down. Be ready to admit your own faults and mistakes.

If all else fails, seek out an impartial third party.

If direct conversation doesn't resolve the conflict, try to engage with someone both parties trust. This can help clarify your positions and bring understanding.

Build toward forgiveness and renewed friendship.

Agree upon how you will communicate to prevent future misunderstandings.

Be Aware

- Seemingly unrelated events in your or another's life may be playing an invisible role in the conflict at hand. Be ready to shift the focus to the real cause, which may not be as it first appears.

- You may not be able to resolve the conflict at this time, but don't give up on future opportunities.

HOW TO WORK FOR WORLD PEACE

Like many Christians, Episcopalians have a passion for bringing Christ's peace into the world. Sometimes that has gotten them into trouble—even with the church! In 1918, Bishop of Utah Paul Jones was driven into resignation, due to the unpopularity of his pacifist views with his fellow bishops. Today his life is commemorated with a place on the church's calendar. The church has come a long way, and these days clergy and lay people are working hand in hand on some exciting and important projects. Here are just a few of them:

The Episcopal Church coordinates ministries we use to carry out the promises we make in our Baptismal Covenant (see page 228), specifically to "strive for justice and peace . . . and respect the dignity of every human being." Check the web at *episcopalchurch. org/page/global-justice*. There you will find links to a number of ongoing programs, including partnership with the ONE Campaign.

Episcopalians for Global Reconciliation is a relatively young grassroots organization serving as a clearinghouse for practical information on improving the world. This group organizes fund drives and special events to involve Episcopalians and their parishes in their on-going work.

Another important grassroots organization is the Episcopal Peace Fellowship. This group advocates on many justice issues, including war and the death penalty. Check them out at *epfnational.org*.

WHAT ARE THE MILLENNIUM DEVELOPMENT GOALS?

They're life-saving, world-changing, and, most importantly, doable.

The eight Millennium Development Goals (MDGs) were set by the United Nations in 2000. They're tangible targets to make significant progress toward solving the world's most pressing problems by the year 2015. One hundred eighty-nine nations have signed on (including the United States), and the General Convention of the Episcopal Church endorsed them in 2003. The MDGs are:

Goal 1: Eradicate extreme poverty and hunger.

Goal 2: Achieve universal primary education.

Goal 3: Promote gender equality and empower women.

Goal 4: Reduce child mortality.

Goal 5: Improve maternal health.

Goal 6: Combat HIV/AIDS, malaria, and other diseases.

Goal 7: Ensure environmental sustainability.

Goal 8: Develop a global partnership for development.

The Episcopal Church made the MDGs a priority. Some parishes are partnering by pledging seven-tenths of 1 percent of their budgets toward funding these goals. Episcopalians are also actively lobbying our government to do the same thing. Find out more at *un.org/millenniumgoals.*

WHERE TO FIND A TRUSTWORTHY RELIEF AGENCY

We all hear the complaints about not-for-profit agencies that spend so much on overhead and marketing that only pennies on the dollar end up going to the cause.

Episcopalians are proud to say that is not the case with our most prominent aid agency, Episcopal Relief and Development (ERD). For more than 70 years, ERD (and its predecessor the Presiding Bishop's Fund for World Relief) has served the needs of the poor and vulnerable, at home and worldwide. Audits show that nearly 90 percent of donated funds go directly toward the relief programs. ERD is able to do this because investment income and shared administration costs with the Episcopal Church cover much of the overhead, which allows donors to know that their gifts, for the most part, go directly to the need. ERD continues to receive a high rating from Charity Navigator for its management and accountability.

From a practical point of view, working through existing church structures is often the best way to help in time of disaster. Unlike other agencies that may not have strong ties to an area, churches already have buildings and relationships with those affected so that more resources can be go directly to meet the need.

ERD has 3,000 volunteers in its network who donate time in a variety of ways. If you have disaster expertise and would like to pitch in here or overseas, contact ERD at *episcopalrelief.org.*

HOW TO GO TO HEAVEN IF YOU'RE RICH

Episcopalians aren't the only ones who wonder about this—it's something every Christian needs to consider. Americans in particular make up less than 5 percent of the world's population yet use about 30 percent of its resources. We live in an undeniably rich country. While much of the world dies of starvation, some of our biggest health problems stem from obesity. And this is bound to raise important questions about our religion. After all, Jesus talked a lot about money.

Believe it or not, next to the kingdom of God, money is the *most* frequent topic Jesus discussed. In the New Testament, one in every 16 verses deals with the subjects of poverty, wealth, injustice, oppression—and God's response to these. In the first three Gospels, it's one in every ten verses. In the book of Luke, it's one in seven.

We all know that money has an alluring and enticing side, one that can so excite us with possessions and experiences that we unwittingly turn a blind eye to our responsibilities to others. Money and possessions can become idols and false gods. This is not to say that Christians cannot (or should not) be rich. Money is not inherently bad, but it is dangerous. Those who have much are responsible for sharing it with those who have little. There is enough money in the world for everyone's need, but not for everyone's greed. Being a true follower of Jesus, as he himself suggested, may not depend so much on how much we *have,* as how much we share.

HOW EPISCOPALIANS ENGAGE CONGRESS

You mean the Episcopal Church is involved in politics?

Of course, and we have been for quite a while. As with many Christian bodies, the Episcopal Church has an established presence in Washington, DC, in the form of the Office of Government Relations, which coordinates with the Episcopal Public Policy Network (EPPN). The EPPN is made up of some 20,000 Episcopalians from around the country who bring the positions of the Episcopal Church to our nation's lawmakers. The social policies established by General Convention and Executive Council include positions on international peace and justice, human rights, immigration, welfare, poverty, violence, and much more.

The Office of Government Relations staff meets regularly with government leaders, works with media, and forms both religious and secular coalitions to further the Church's social policies. Episcopalians establish these policies when we gather every three years in General Convention. This is when we pass resolutions urging action in a number of different areas, such as increasing aid to war-torn areas or urging disarmament of nuclear weapons.

EPPN sees its work as an extension of our Baptismal Covenant (see page 222) as we "strive for justice and peace among all people." You can learn more (and join!) by contacting EPPN at *episcopal.grassroots.com*.

HOW EPISCOPALIANS EVANGELIZE

To some Episcopalians it is known as the "E" word.

Perhaps it's because many of us come from backgrounds where "evangelism" and "evangelical" have narrow meanings. Episcopalians have nothing against sharing our faith with others; it's just that we tend to do it differently than those who are more vocal about it.

Episcopalians understand that sharing our faith is not optional, it's a long-standing biblical command, and it's something we take very seriously. Episcopalians tend to see their evangelism as something much deeper than simply getting people into church. That's why we tend to shy away from emotion-charged worship that can be interpreted as high-powered sales pitches. We see salvation as a journey and a process, not just a one-time event. Archbishop of Canterbury William Temple once put it this way, "I have been saved, I am being saved, and I will be saved."

Many Episcopalians link evangelism with the two commandments Jesus gave us, to love God and to love our neighbors. We believe that in loving our neighbor, Christ is revealed. And it is he who really does the work, though not without human helpers. So our most successful strategy involves being ourselves, loving and listening to people, praying for them, and being whatever help we can. It means being a friend and family to those around us.

Small acts of evangelism and sharing of Christ's love with others can bring people into that love, summed up in the motto, "The Episcopal Church welcomes you." The hospitality, open-mindedness, and welcome that Episcopalians try to embody encompass our deepest expression of evangelism. And we believe this is what truly resonates with those who are searching for God.

Sharing God by loving others is at the heart of how Episcopalians evangelize.

HOW EPISCOPALIANS MAKE DISCIPLES

One of the last things Jesus told those who would follow him was this: "Go therefore and make disciples of all nations" (Matthew 28:1). Jesus seemed intent on having Christians go forward and not simply tell people who he was, but to bring people into a deeper understanding of and participation in his life and teaching.

Different Christian traditions do this in many different ways. Episcopalians do it in part through worship—the first step in mission. Since worship is about the endless work of giving thanks, this is a task that involves everything we are. Episcopal worship revolves around regular times of prayer and culminates in our Sunday celebration of Holy Eucharist. During the week, the Book of Common Prayer recommends we give thanks to God at Morning Prayer (page 75) and Evening Prayer (page 115). There are other opportunities for worship at other times of the day (noon, at meals, and before bed) that are also included in the Prayer Book. All are designed to help us be the thankful, generous-hearted, and Christ-centered people we want to be.

At Sunday worship, we engage in the work of discipleship by gathering together to hear the Bible proclaimed and interpreted, and to take part in that mystical and mysterious liturgy of Holy Communion. This was the most profound act of worship Jesus taught his disciples. On the night before he died, Jesus took bread and broke it, took wine and shared it, as his Body and Blood given for us. When we partake of his Body and Blood, we are empowered to break open our lives and pour them out in love to a hurting world. At the end of the Eucharistic liturgy we are sent forth into the world empowered to follow Christ *in* that world, to love and serve those not yet part of our church family. In a sense, the church itself breathes the Holy Spirit in and out as disciples make disciples.

WHY (SOME OF) OUR CHURCH DOORS ARE RED

Some call it tradition; others think it's just a snappy-looking color. But the deeper reason is the firm belief that our churches are places of refuge.

As is the case with many churches, Episcopal parishes use red to let the world know what we're about. Red is the color of Christ's blood. It is the symbol of the sacrifice of the martyrs. It is the symbol of the presence of the Holy Spirit. And it marks the holy ground that lies just within. We like to think that red tells the world we're a safe place. We're a peaceful place. We're a place of refuge. We are a place where God's presence is made clear.

Historically, churches painted their doors red to signal fleeing suspects that they were places of sanctuary (thank King Ethelbert's English law, circa 600 CE). Today we know that the world is a scary place, full of people who are looking for places to find peace and forgiveness. While many people look at traditional churches as daunting and inhospitable, we hope that our red doors tell a different story, even if circumstances require they be locked from time to time!

Many people come to the Episcopal Church from other traditions, and some have had bad church experiences that have left them scarred or leery about God and God's people. We know that churches are not clubs for saints but hospitals for sinners. So just as hospitals display a red cross, we also like to announce that we are a place of healing and restoration. At our best, our parishes help the wounded put their lives back together, provide comfort in time of need, and the doors open wide to welcome people in.

HOW TO TELL A SINNER FROM A SAINT

Many Christians claim they can tell the difference between saints and sinners. Sinners are naughty and do naughty things, they say, and saints are nice and do nice things. For Episcopalians, however, who strive to seek and serve Christ in all persons, distinguishing saint from sinner has never been easy. Since you likely know yourself better than anyone else, it is good to start there rather than on others.

Grapple briefly with the following question: "Can the finite bear the infinite?"

Originally used by the church to help resolve the debate over whether Jesus was only human or only divine, this question can be useful when discerning sinner from saint. Episcopalians answer the question by saying, "Yes!" Baptism makes the finite (you) able to bear the infinite (Christ), so it's not a matter of naughty or nice, sinner or saint (or, in Jesus' case, man or God). A person is fully a saint and fully a sinner at the same time, just as Jesus is one person, fully human and fully divine.

Embrace the sinner, and the saint will be revealed.

Fearlessly and truthfully answer the question, "Am I a sinner?" based strictly on the evidence at hand. (Hint: when in doubt simply measure yourself against the Ten Commandments.)

Learn what the Scripture says about it.

Scripture makes clear that being a sinner is a prerequisite for being a saint (see Romans 5:8; Galatians 2:17; and Matthew 9:13). Why else would a saint "boast" that he was himself the chief of sinners (1 Timothy 1:15)? Why else would anyone confess, "I do not do the good I want but the evil I do not want is what I do"? (Romans 7:19).

Be Aware

Although Christians are exhorted to "tame the flesh," they can't make themselves "less of a sinner" over time. You can't become, say, 35 percent sinner and 65 percent saint if you just work really hard at it. You can't change the percentages of sinner/saint within you. The message of grace is to be a sinner who has been forgiven, by accepting God's forgiveness. When each of us falls, as no doubt we will, the goal is to get up again. Martin Luther once said that we were "simultaneously sinners and justified." The fact that we have been forgiven indicates we had something that needed forgiveness. (Reflect on Romans 5:6–10.) The grace of that forgiveness comes from the overflowing of God's love—as a gift, not something we deserve. It is no accident that the Lord's Prayer, geared as it is to "daily" use, also reminds us to pray for forgiveness every day, and to forgive others in the same way.

TEN IMPORTANT EPISCOPAL MISSIONARIES AND WHAT THEY DID

Domestic

Jonathan Myrick Daniels

A seminary student from New England, Daniels was a missionary in the South during the struggle for civil rights. In 1965, Daniels was among those responding to Martin Luther King, Jr.'s call to protest in Alabama, when he was shot outside a grocery store while protecting an African-American teen. His death, at age 26, helped awaken Americans to the seriousness of the civil rights challenge in the United States.

Jackson Kemper

The first missionary bishop of the Episcopal Church, Kemper left his native New York to found missions in the Midwest. In 1835, Kemper headed west to found, among other things, a college in St. Louis, Missouri, a seminary in Racine, Wisconsin, and a mission parish in Milwaukee that stands today as the Cathedral Church of All Saints.

Thomas Gallaudet

Known as "missionary to the deaf," Gallaudet carried on a family tradition. The son of Thomas H. Gallaudet, who helped found the first institution for the education of the deaf in North America, young Thomas founded a church and school for the deaf. One of his students, Henry Winter Syle, became the first deaf person ordained in the Episcopal Church.

David Pendleton Oakerhater

A Native American, Oakerhater was a warrior and leader of the Cheyenne in Oklahoma. Following his capture and conversion to

Christianity while incarcerated, Oakerhater became a deacon and then returned to his people. As a missionary to the Cheyenne, Oakerhater founded several schools and missions.

Caroline Louise Darling

It sometimes comes as a surprise to learn that the Episcopal Church has nuns (see the next chapter). Darling is just one of many religious sisters who have served the church. Better known by her religious name, Sister Constance, she and other Sisters of Saint Mary ministered in nineteenth-century Memphis to those stricken by yellow fever. She, her sisters, and other faithful ministers remained to care for the sick and dying during the epidemics, as droves of people were moving out. In 1878, when an epidemic killed more than 5,000 people, Constance, three other nuns, and two priests joined the number of those who perished at their posts. They are remembered today as "The Martyrs of Memphis."

Foreign

James Holly

Born to freed slaves in Washington, DC, James Theodore Holly was the first African-American ordained as an Episcopal bishop, as a missionary bishop of Haiti. He had served at St. Luke's in New Haven, Connecticut, where in 1856 he founded the Protestant Episcopal Society for Promoting the Extension of the Church Among Colored People, which eventually became the Union of Black Episcopalians (*ube.org*).

Channing Moore Williams

How does a poor farm boy grow up to be a bearer of the Gospel halfway round the world? One answer is the Holy Spirit, coupled with willingness to look into your heart. Williams presented himself as a missionary for work in China, where he was ordained in 1857. Soon after he was assigned to Japan, and eventually became Missionary Bishop in China and Japan. He translated much of the BCP into Japanese, and founded a university in Edo (now

Tokyo). He also helped join the diverse missions of English and American workers into a unified "Holy Catholic Church of Japan" (*Nippon Sei Ko Kai*)—one of the member churches of the Anglican Communion.

Samuel Isaac Joseph Schereschewsky

Born in Lithuania to Jewish parents in 1831, Schereschewsky originally studied to be a rabbi but became acquainted with Christianity when he encountered a Hebrew translation of the New Testament. He became an Episcopalian and, after ordination, responded to a call for help in the mission field of China. With a gift for languages, he translated the Bible and parts of the BCP into Mandarin. Upon Bishop Williams' transfer to Japan, he was chosen as Bishop of Shanghai. He began translations of the Scripture and Prayer Book into Wenli, but was stricken with paralysis and resigned his episcopate. He continued to translate, typing over 2,000 pages with the finger of one hand, calling it "the work for which I am best fitted." He died in 1906 and is buried in Tokyo.

Lucien Lee Kinsolving and James Watson Morris

Kinsolving and Morris were Episcopal missionaries to Brazil. They held the first service on Trinity Sunday 1890 in Porto Alegre. Within a year, three additional missionaries—William Cabell Brown, John Gaw Meem, and Mary Packard—arrived and joined the work. These five missionaries are considered the founders of the Episcopal Anglican Church of Brazil. In 1899, Kinsolving was made missionary bishop for the work in Brazil by the House of Bishops of the Episcopal Church, and in 1907 the missionary district of Brazil was established by the General Convention. Today the church in Brazil is a member of the Anglican Communion.

Samuel David Ferguson

While most overseas Episcopal missionary work was in Central and South America and the Far East, Episcopalians also made their mark in Africa. Ferguson was born in South Carolina in 1842 but emigrated to Liberia with his family as a child. He studied and became a teacher in the Episcopal mission school, was ordained and served a parish church in Harper, Liberia. Eventually he was chosen as Bishop of Cape Palmas, which later became the Diocese of Liberia. He is remembered as the founder of Cuttington College, now a university carrying forth the educational mission Ferguson envisioned.

MONKS AND NUNS
AND FRIARS, OH MY!

Many people are surprised to learn that some Anglicans, including Episcopalians, choose to live as part of what are known as *religious communities*. Though many know that Henry VIII closed down most of the English monasteries, few know that he also founded two others. (Henry was a quirky character, but then, people were not likely to point out his inconsistencies to his face!) It is safe to say that "religious life" (life lived under vows of poverty, chastity, and obedience, usually in community) was at a low ebb in England from the time of Henry's dissolution of the monasteries. However, note should be taken of the small community of Anglicans gathered at Little Gidding, under the guidance of Deacon Nicholas Ferrar, in the early seventeenth century. While not strictly monastic (in that the community included married couples and their children), Little Gidding served as an inspiration not only to the revival of religious communities in the nineteenth century, but to poet T.S. Eliot, who devoted the last of his *Four Quartets* to that small group of faithful Christian witnesses.

The religious life revived in England and America in the nineteenth century with the foundation of a number of sisterhoods and brotherhoods, some monastic and geared to a life of common prayer (monks and nuns) but some directed more toward external service and works of mercy such as teaching, nursing, or missionary work (sisters and brothers, the latter sometimes called "friars"). Many of these communities have adapted the traditional rules of life from Benedict, Augustine, Dominic, Francis, and Vincent de Paul. Others have crafted new models of life and ministry, some of them in this and the last century by adapting the traditional vows to new forms of Christian community. Today the Anglican Communion boasts almost a hundred communities of men or women (or mixed communities of both), many of them either begun in America or with American branches. Their members number from a handful to scores.

So the next time you see a monk, nun, sister, or friar in a habit, don't assume them to be Roman Catholic. They may very well be one of our own!

HOW TO BECOME A MISSIONARY (SHORT TERM)

Adventure, intrigue, and service—there are plenty of reasons people choose to help others through short-term work in the mission field.

The Episcopal Church offers numerous opportunities for mission. The Young Adult Service Corps provides assignments typically one year long, and offers guided reflection and mentoring. Take a look at *episcopalchurch.org/page/young-adult-service-corps*.

Volunteers might work as teachers in music, English, math, or religion. They also may work providing supervision in homes for young girls or as building project supervisors, serve as community development workers, set up computer networks and financial management systems, and much more.

The Episcopal Church looks for committed Christians who feel called to the task and are physically and mentally strong. Volunteers are usually active in their congregations and dioceses and are eager to work in partnership with others.

Of course, there are many local opportunities for service and mission, so be sure to contact your congregation's clergy and the diocesan office. Your own hometown might be where your mission calls you!

HOW TO BECOME A MISSIONARY (LONG TERM)

So you want to make it a career?

Those who serve for three years or longer in the mission field for the Episcopal Church are typically called Appointed Missionaries. These folks take on many of the same tasks as short-term missionaries (such as the YASCers of the Young Adult Service Corps); however, their terms are longer, renewable, and include financial support from the Episcopal Church.

Life in the mission field is not for the faint of heart. Not only does it require the physical and mental strength to deal with separation from the home environment, but it also requires a deep spirituality. This means that your central task as a missionary is to love the people whom you encounter. Missionaries undertake an array of life-giving tasks, but the most important is to show forth Christ's love.

Appointees often have advanced degrees in theology, missiology, or a field related to their work. Their tasks may include medicine, social work, and development. Nearly 100 men and women are currently engaged in mission work of this kind. They see their work of partnering with indigenous people as a way to live out their Baptismal Covenant (see page 222).

If you're interested in finding out more, contact the head of Mission Personnel at "Mission Central"—*episcopalchurch.org/page/mission-personnel.*

WHAT IS THE ANGLICAN COMMUNION AND HOW DO I JOIN?

The Episcopal Church is one of 44 national and regional churches or jurisdictions in 165 countries worldwide that make up the Anglican Communion (see the list on page 199). We're more than 80 million members strong.

We are a loosely based fellowship held together by Jesus Christ and the distinctive beliefs we share, largely as they were spread in the expansion of the British Empire (and later by Americans) and the church that traveled with them, bringing along the Book of Common Prayer. The Communion has no central government, but is loosely linked by four "instruments" of communion: the **Archbishop of Canterbury**, with headquarters at Lambeth Palace in London; this residence gives its name to the **Lambeth Conference**, a once-a-decade meeting (since 1867) of bishops from around the world to discuss matters of common concern; the **Primates' Meeting**, a smaller and more frequent gathering of the senior bishop from each of the churches; and the **Anglican Consultative Council**, a representative body of bishops, clergy, and lay leaders from all of the churches, primarily focused on the mission work of the whole Anglican Communion. In recent years, the Communion has adopted *indaba* as a way of working. What's that? See the next section!

The Anglican Communion is the third-largest Christian body in the world. This means that practically anywhere you go you'll find a church that shares a common history. All of these churches have Prayer Books, often written and adapted by each local body, adding a richness and distinctiveness reflective of each culture. Members of one church will be welcome in another, regardless of the country (or continent). Joining the Episcopal Church automatically makes you a member of the Anglican Communion.

The Anglican Communion website is *anglicancommunion.org.*

WHAT IS INDABA?

Indaba is a Zulu word that describes a way of engaging in dialogue and discernment that is profoundly respectful of differences. It can be thought of more as "living together" than "solving problems."

In 2008, the bishops gathered at the Lambeth Conference were invited to participate in this form of conversation, in part to address tensions and stresses that had developed in the Communion over the prior decades. Many of the bishops found the experience fruitful, and the idea of continuing the method and sharing it more widely came to bear fruit in what is called "The Continuing Indaba." This is a process of dialogue and experience in which representatives from churches in three different parts of the world visit each other's areas and learn of their experiences, intensifying the conversation rather than avoiding it. It combines theological reflection as well as biblical study, and sharing personal perspectives and insights. The goal is to use *difference* as a source of energy for mission, rather than as an obstacle.

In addition to the use of Indaba on an international scale, it has also been applied across and within dioceses as a way to encourage conversation and strengthen mission. You can learn more at *continuingindaba.com.*

TEN BEAUTIFUL EPISCOPAL CHURCHES

Beauty is in the eye of the beholder, of course. Nonetheless, here are ten very different and lovely examples of the wide variety of architectural styles as seen in Episcopal churches—one from each province of the Episcopal Church and the Convocation of Episcopal Churches in Europe. Look them up online, or visit them if you find yourself nearby.

Province I:

St. Andrew's, Newcastle, Maine

Province II:

Grace Church, Manhattan

Province III:

The Washington National Cathedral

Province IV:
Holy Trinity, Vicksburg, Mississippi

Province V:
Church of the Atonement, Fish Creek, Wisconsin

Province VI:
Cathedral of Our Merciful Saviour, Faribault, Minnesota

Province VII:
Grace Cathedral, Topeka, Kansas

Province VIII:
Grace Church, Bainbridge Island, Washington

Province IX:
Catedral de el Señor, Quito, Ecuador

Convocation of Episcopal Churches in Europe:
Church of the Ascension, Munich, Germany

WHY THE EPISCOPAL CHURCH WELCOMES EVERYONE

Like many Christians, Episcopalians see Jesus' central message as reconciliation—repairing and restoring relationships among people and between people and God. In fact, that's how we define the mission of the church: "to restore all people to unity with God and each other in Christ" (BCP 855). When Jesus came to do this work, he didn't surround himself with people who thought they had their act together, pious rabbis or society's upper crust. Jesus spent an inordinate amount of time hanging out with tradespeople, prostitutes, tax collectors, women—the comfortable and hard-working as well as the marginalized and outcast. Jesus famously said that healthy people don't need doctors, sick people do.

Episcopalians take this to heart. We see Jesus' proclivity to invite everyone, and not turn anybody away. We like to think we welcome everyone because Jesus does.

Welcoming everyone does not mean we have no rules, boundaries, or guidelines. What it means is that we hope—and work—to be slow to judge and condemn. After all, one of Jesus' strongest warnings was not to judge (Matthew 7:1). Judgment is up to God. And when the verdict comes in, we believe God's mercy will win out over God's judgment—for us, too. This is why we believe that showing God's acceptance, forgiveness, love, and welcome should be our defining characteristics, as this is how we hope to be treated ourselves.

Episcopalians betray their optimism in the very first line of our Catechism (BCP 845). When asked, "What are we by nature?" our first answer is not, "We are reprobate sinners in the hands of an angry God," but, "We are part of God's creation, made in the image of God." It's not that Episcopalians dismiss sin (look just two questions further into the Catechism!), it's that we believe that Jesus' power to overcome human transgressions and bring forgiveness is more powerful than any sin. The Gospel of reconciliation makes Episcopalians a hopeful people who love to laugh, celebrate, and welcome everyone to the party—which means you're invited, too.

BIBLE STUFF

Including some hot questions about what the Bible says and how the Episcopal Church understands it

HOW EPISCOPALIANS READ THE BIBLE (AND WHY MORE SHOULD)

It's the best-selling book of all time—but perhaps the least read.

A 2014 survey by the American Bible Society reveals that 88 percent of American households own a Bible (and the average American home has 4.7 copies at hand), but only 37 percent of Americans read from one of them more than once a week. It is hard to tell how many people think Joan of Arc was Noah's wife, but the percentage of Americans who believe the Bible is sacred is down to 79 percent from 86 percent just three years earlier. The number of the devout and the skeptics is tied at 19 percent each; and 26 percent of Americans never read the Bible, climbing to 39 percent of the Millennial group. While Episcopalians probably score about average, it's not for lack of exposure, or a definite interpretive model toward understanding the Holy Scriptures.

Even if Episcopalians don't read the Bible privately, we are exposed to considerable portions of it corporately, in worship. The Lectionary (the selection of Scripture readings appointed for Sunday worship) spreads out considerable portions of the Bible in a three-year cycle. Those who follow the Daily Office (corporately or as a private devotion) will read even more of the Scripture.

When it comes to interpretation, Episcopalians have two rules, whether as part of worship or read privately. As children of the English Reformation, which brought us the English Bible, we are strong believers in everyone's ability to read and interpret Scripture. We like to think that the observations of the farmhand, the homemaker, the nurse, and the auto mechanic are integral to arriving at what it is the Scriptures are saying to us.

However, we also believe there is a place for reasoned, informed, and educated reflection on the matter. When we read the Bible, we are apt to do so alongside a study book called a commentary. We also think it fitting to hold and attend classes that expose us to the breadth of Bible scholarship available. And Episcopalians believe in and rely on an educated clergy who go through an extensive educational program—usually though not solely at the graduate level in seminary. Parishioners often look to clergy as resources for Bible interpretation.

Despite these convictions, Episcopalians are usually the first ones to admit we're not Bible experts, and we can always learn. There is a wonderful quotation attributed to St. Gregory the Great (to whom it could be said we owe our Anglican existence, since he is the one who sent St. Augustine to Canterbury): "The Bible is a stream in which a lamb may wade while an elephant swims." Many of us think we should read the Bible more often, whether wading or swimming. And many of us are thankful that we have many resources at hand should we decide to do so. Although we still wouldn't know who Noah's wife was; the Bible never names her.

WHO WROTE THE BIBLE?

The Bible is not a book, but a collection of books—and different churches include different numbers of them, though most agree on 66 of the Old and New Testaments (up to 18 books of the Apocrypha or Deuterocanonical books are included by some as part of the Old Testament). These different books were written by dozens of authors, and reached the form in which we know them after the work of many editors and copyists. These books span more than a thousand years and include many different genres such as history, poetry, wisdom, and prophecy. It's no surprise that each book has its own story of authorship and "redaction" (the fancy word for editing), and thanks to the depth of antiquity we simply don't have answers to a lot of important questions. Biblical scholars have attempted to reconstruct and tease apart the various layers of authorship (and redaction), and while there is some general agreement about some portions of Scripture, there is significant disagreement about others.

While some Christians believe that the Bible was inerrantly written by the hand of God, Episcopalians tend to see it differently. We believe that God *inspired* the human authors, and speaks to us through what they wrote, not that God *dictated*. There are a few portions of Scripture where the human author does record having been told, "Write this . . ." (such as Exodus 17:14 and Revelation 14:13). But the fact that the author goes out of the way to note that instruction demonstrates it is not universal. Actual divine writing is limited to instances such as the Ten Commandments and the "handwriting on the wall" in Daniel 5. As to humans, St. Paul takes the time to spell out when he's offering his own opinion and has *not* been instructed by God (1 Corinthians 7:12).

So when we say the Bible is "the Word of God," we mean it comes from God both by inspiration and understanding. God inspired people to write and continues to speak to us through what they wrote, as we engage with it and understand it. Thus the biases, preferences, and prejudices of the authors and the readers, as well as their and our cultural understandings, are present in the final result. There is widely agreed-upon evidence of rearrangement, addition, and subtraction in the compilation of our most sacred book, including the continued debate between the churches as to the status of the Apocrypha—whether they are in the Bible or not. This does not make the Bible any less "true," but it does help us better understand the human side of the work by which it came to be.

We do know that the Bible was primarily written within two communities, ancient Israel and the emerging Christian Church. Both of these large groupings contained many subdivisions with their own traditions and concerns. In the nineteenth century, scholars began to notice some of the seams and duplications in the five books traditionally attributed to Moses, and theorized at least four different strands of thought woven together in the final product. Scholarship suggests that the Gospels (Matthew, Mark, Luke, and John) were similarly products not so much of the named individuals, but of and for the communities of their own disciples and followers. There is no doubt that holy men and women, moved by God, participated in bringing these great writings to us. So we tend to see the Bible's origins less as divine authorship and more as a human response to the presence and action of God. To use an analogy from computer science, it is "written once, read many times." And each reading may bring some new insight.

So we believe God still speaks to us through what once was written. While we're not about to suggest any additions to the Bible (though there are many editions!), we are alert to ways the Living God continues to inform us and communicate with us. Our quest for authorship is ongoing, as is our search for the ways God continues to speak and actively move in our lives.

Some like to think of the Bible as historical, metaphorical, and sacramental. It is historical, meaning it is a product of its time, as well as in part a record of events. But, as with all history, the accounts it gives point beyond that mere record of events into a metaphorical understanding; this helps get beyond questions of literal fact and into deeper truths. Finally, it is sacramental, in that it mediates the sacred, working as a vehicle of the Holy Spirit in our lives.

Episcopalians don't tend merely to take the Bible literally, or to treat it as inerrant, but we do take it seriously. This includes paying attention to the latest archaeological findings as well as the ongoing studies of the transmission of texts. All of these help us understand the history and origins of the Scriptures.

COMMON TRANSLATIONS OF THE BIBLE

As noted on the previous page, there are many editions of the Bible. Even the original Hebrew, Aramaic, and Greek texts appeared in hundreds of manuscripts, many of them fragmentary, and the work of rabbis, scholars, and theologians pieced them together into more or less rational editions. You can purchase copies of such "original language" versions, and in them you will see the copious footnotes that reveal the thousands of variant readings, omissions, and additions.

Of course, most of us don't know the ancient languages in which the Scriptures were written, so we rely on translations. The translators themselves will have to make choices as to which reading to use from the many manuscript variants, and how to put those words into a different language. There are two basic approaches to translation:

Formal equivalence strives as much as possible to give a word-for-word recreation of the original, preserving some of the grammatical features of the original language. This can produce an awkward result from time to time, and also faces the difficulty of individual words in Hebrew or Greek simply not having an English equivalent, as rich as English is in its vocabulary. The translators of the Authorized Version (the "King James Version") took this approach, and helpfully italicized words they felt constrained to add in order to make sense. (Hebrew, for example, doesn't always use forms of the verb *to be*; so the KJV prints the first line of Psalm 23 as "The Lord *is* my shepherd. . . .")

Dynamic equivalence tends to translate thought-for-thought and, rather than preserving original word order (for example), aims to produce an effect on English readers similar to what the readers of the original text would have felt in their own language. This generally makes for easier reading, both silently and aloud.

Some versions take the process even further, and become **paraphrases** of the original. Examples include *The Living Bible* and *The Message.* In these the authors (who may not really be translators at all) put a good deal of their own reflection into the text. Such paraphrases are not recommended without comparison with real translations, though the freedom of expression and freshness may spark new ideas.

Most translations are made by committee, and a few by dedicated individuals. Both forms of translation have their virtues and faults. Ideally it is wise to have more than one translation at your disposal, perhaps one of the more readable *dynamic* versions for lengthy reading, and a *formal* version to compare passages that raise a question in your mind.

Another point to remember is that some Bibles designed solely for Protestant church use will not include the Apocrypha or Deuterocanonical books. The Episcopal Church does make use of these books in its liturgy, and they form a part of the Bible for Roman Catholics and Eastern Orthodox believers. All of the translations indicated for Roman Catholic use, or produced ecumenically, appear in editions including these texts.

Here are some of the most popular English translations currently available, in chronological order of publication. There are also versions in many other languages, though English seems to have more variety than any other single language. *(Note: **D** indicates a dynamic, idea-based approach; **F** a formal, word-for-word approach.)*

1611 Authorized ("King James") Version (KJV)
Still the "gold standard," this is the "official" translation of Anglicanism, and widely respected beyond it. Noted for the beauty of its language, it is not always easy for a modern reader to understand obsolete words or those that have changed in meaning.

Most editions do not contain the Apocrypha, but the King James version of those books is available separately. **F**

1970 New American Bible (NAB)

The official version used in the Roman Catholic Church in the United States. It is scholarly, but in spite of being intended for worship use, it is sometimes difficult to read aloud. The New Testament was revised in 1986. **F**

1971 New American Standard Bible (NASB)

An update of the 1901 American Standard Version, further updated in 1995. It is still widely used in conservative and evangelical Protestant churches. **F**

1976 Today's English Version (a.k.a. The Good News Bible) (TEV)

This version was among the first composed specifically with a goal to accessibility and as an outreach tool. It was produced by the American Bible Society. The language is deliberately simple, and the text is accompanied by simplified line drawings. **D**

1978 New International Version (NIV)

This is a mainstream Protestant evangelical translation that balances somewhat between **D** and **F**, striving for readability without sacrificing "accuracy." It was revised in 1984 and 2011. It does not include the Apocrypha or Deuterocanonical books.

1982 New King James Version (NKJV)

An effort to update the KJV into more modern English while preserving as much of the older language as possible. **F**

1985 New Jerusalem Bible (NJB)

An update of the 1966 Jerusalem Bible, designed for Roman Catholic use. The earlier edition had verged on paraphrase from time to time, with an eye to the French version that preceded it. The 1985 version sought to return to a more closely **D** approach. It is the most widely used Roman Catholic English version outside of the United States.

1989 Revised English Bible (REB)

This is an update of the 1970 New English Bible, correcting some of its eccentricities. It was produced as an ecumenical effort by Roman Catholic, Anglican, and Protestant churches in Great Britain. It is considered one of the more elegant and readable versions for worship. **D**

1989 New Revised Standard Version (NRSV)

This is an update of the 1952 Revised Standard Version, removing some of the archaic language that had remained in the former version (such as the use of "thee" and "thou" in reference to God). It was produced by the National Council of Churches and has wide support; it includes the Apocrypha, but a decision to use inclusive or gender-neutral language in many passages led the Orthodox Church in America to decline its use in worship. It is the version you are likely to hear in the Episcopal Church's liturgy, and combines the virtues of scholarship and readability. It lies somewhere on the spectrum between **F** and **D** but with the heritage of the former.

1995 Contemporary English Version (CEV)

This is another effort from the American Bible Society, similar to the Good News Bible, to produce a Bible readable at elementary-school level. This makes it very suitable for young readers, but less well suited to Bible study. **D**

2001 English Standard Version (ESV)

This is also a revision of the 1952 Revised Standard Version, but more conservative in its choices, attempting to be as literal as possible, and choosing not to make as many attempts at inclusive or gender-neutral language. It was slightly revised in 2007 and 2011. There is an edition with a version of the Apocrypha, as well as numerous study editions with extensive notes. **F**

2011 Common English Bible (CEB)

A joint effort of Episcopal, Methodist, Presbyterian, and Congregationalist publishers, this version is intended for ease of reading as well as fidelity, with a goal of a seventh-grade reading level. It lies somewhere between **D** and **F**, as the primary goal was readability.

The Canon and the Translations

Title II Canon 2 of the Canons of the Episcopal Church lists which translations of the Scripture are authorized for reading the lessons in public worship. Perhaps needless to say, the Authorized Version (the King James Bible of 1611) is the first authorized, though it is rare to hear it actually used in churches. The version most often heard today is the New Revised Standard Version—and this is the version that appears in most printed lectionaries and books of the Gospels used in worship. The Canon includes most of the modern versions, but shies away from paraphrases and translations that are the work of a single scholar. As new translations are published, the Canon is amended to add them (or not). There is also a provision for the diocesan bishop to authorize the use of translations into languages other than English.

TYPES OF BIBLES AND THEIR FEATURES

It is written in the book of Ecclesiastes, "Of the making of many books there is no end" (12:12). Certainly Bible publishers have taken this to heart. Almost every translation of the Bible comes in multiple editions. Here are a few things to note about the various features, varieties, and editions of Bibles you will likely find in any good book store. Not all features are found with every translation, but most will include one or more.

Including the Apocrypha/Deuterocanonical Books

All Bible versions authorized for use in the Roman Catholic Church (the New American and New Jerusalem, for example) will automatically contain these books, interleaved in their historic position among the books of the Old Testament). Some versions are available with or without, and the package or the spine of the book will usually indicate if the Apocrypha/Deuterocanonicals are included, usually in a separate section between the Old and New Testaments.

Study and Focus Bibles

- A **Study Bible** includes overviews and introductory articles to each book, and usually has extensive footnotes or other commentary. Not to be confused with the occasional note in some versions indicating alternate translations, these notes give more historical and interpretative context. These often include extensive charts, maps, and tables.

- **Focus or Devotional Bibles** will have articles or notes geared to particular audiences. Sometimes the edition will only include the New Testament (sometimes with the Book of Psalms). There are literally hundreds of such editions: for Men, for Women, for the Military, for Doctors, for Teens, and on and on. These are often gift items, which may go toward the 4.7 Bibles in the average American home!

One Year Bible

Arranged for reading the whole Bible in a single year. (See page 155 for other ideas about reading the Bible in a year.)

Parallel Bible

These editions will have two or more translations side by side for comparison. They are very useful and convenient for Bible study.

Children's Bible

Usually an illustrated, abridged version of the Bible, sometimes in simplified language. Be aware that some take a rather strong sectarian point of view in deciding what to include or omit; and remembering that a picture is worth a thousand words, be aware of the messages sent and received through the illustrations.

Concordance Bible

Has a dictionary or abridged concordance in which you can find a verse by looking up a key word. Full concordances of specific versions are also available.

Cross Reference Bible

Editors provide links between verses based either on citation (as when a Gospel passage refers to the Law or the Prophets) or on topical similarity. The links usually appear in the margin, footnote, or a center column. The "chain reference" system will lead you from verse to verse.

Red Letter Bible

The words of Jesus are printed in red or another contrasting color.

Self-Pronouncing Bible

Unusual or uncommon words are marked with diacritical signs and accent marks (as in a dictionary) to assist in pronunciation.

Software

In addition to all of the print Bibles, many versions are also available either online or as part of computer programs such as

Hermeneutika's *BibleWorks* or the Logos Bible Software. Some versions are even available as apps for smartphones and tablets—as is the Book of Common Prayer itself!

Audio and Large Print

A number of Bible translations are available as audio (usually on CD or as audio files) or in larger print and Braille for the visually impaired.

HOW TO CHOOSE A BIBLE THAT'S RIGHT FOR YOU

So, given all of the translations and the options provided by the many editions from the many Bible publishers, how do you go about making a choice for something as important as engaging with God's Word? Choosing wisely can lead to a lifetime relationship with the Scriptures.

Know yourself and your motivations.

Think about who you are and why you want to explore the Bible. Do you need a simple Bible or a more nuanced translation? Is this Bible for devotional use or for in-depth study? Do you need one with lots of pictures or are you happy with just the text?

Find a Bible translation in a language you speak and that speaks to you.

If you are comfortable in the world of Elizabethan England, you might get a good deal out of the Authorized Version. Otherwise, you might want to consider a more recent translation, including one of those using the "thought-for-thought" approach, which tend to be easier to read.

Seek a translation rather than a paraphrase.

A paraphrase is a rewording of the Bible, an interpretation of a translation. This is like making a photocopy of a photocopy; resolution and clarity start to diminish, and the opinions of the one doing the paraphrase will loom large. Look on the title page or preface for a phrase like "translated from the original languages" if you want to avoid a paraphrase.

Check on the translators' forthrightness in revealing their choices.

Look for footnotes offering alternative translations or that point out where the biblical texts are difficult and the meaning uncertain. Translators always make choices, sometimes tough ones;

good translations clue you in when other possible meanings are available, or the "literal" text says something (for instance, using a metaphor that doesn't speak to modern ears) that needs some nuance. A good translation will tell you when it has done that.

Read a familiar passage as a test.

Can you understand what you are reading? Does it help you hear God's word anew? Consider a passage other than John 3:16 or Psalm 23.

Unless you can read biblical Hebrew, Aramaic, and Greek, you might want to find yourself a good translation in a language you understand.

Clarify your need for "helps."

Does the translation include introductions and explanations? Such comments are not a part of the Bible, but can be a real plus in understanding the text, especially for serious study. Some study Bibles use call-outs, sidebars, and discussion questions to add another dimension to Scripture reading.

Be Aware

- God speaks to us through the Bible. Reading an accurate, understandable translation can result in radical life transformations, spiritual maturity, and actual growth in faith.

- A number of Bible versions are available as apps for smartphones and other devices, a handy way always to have the Scripture available.

HOW TO READ THE BIBLE

So now that you've got your Bible, what do you do with it? The Bible is not a single book but a library: a collection of at least 66 separate books gathered together over hundreds of years and thousands of miles. Divided into the Old Testament (originally in Hebrew and Aramaic, and in the Intertestamental Apocrypha and Deuterocanonicals, Greek) and the New Testament (Greek), these writings have many authors and take many forms. What some churches call the Apocrypha or Deuterocanonical books are part of the Old Testament for others.

The Bible includes histories, stories, letters, prophecies, poems, dreams or visions and their interpretations, songs, teachings, and laws, to name a few categories. Christians believe the Bible is an account of God's relationship with humankind and a powerful way that God speaks to people. So how do you join in that conversation?

Determine your purpose for reading.

Clarify in your own mind what you hope to gain. Your motivations should be well intentioned, such as to seek information, to gain a deeper understanding of God and yourself, or to enrich your faith. Pray for insight before every reading time.

Resolve to read daily.

Commit to a daily regimen of Bible reading. Make it a part of your routine until it becomes a habit.

Master the mechanics.

- Learn the order in which the books are placed. Most folks can say, "Matthew, Mark, Luke, and John,"

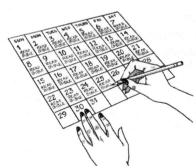

Commit to reading the Bible daily.

but it is good to remember that the Hebrew Scriptures follow the basic division of Law, Writings, and Prophets. The Epistles (Letters) attributed to Paul are in order based on length. (Not the way we'd order things these days!)

- Familiarize yourself with the introductory material. Many Bible translations include helpful information at the front of the Bible and at the beginning of each book.
- The books are broken down into chapters and verses. These are a later addition to the text but make things much easier when it comes to references. There are some slight numbering differences between some of the versions, but those differences will usually be noted.
- If your Bible contains maps (usually in the back), consult them when

chapter
number
↓

Proverbs 26:11

↗   ↑
book   verse
name   number

cities, mountains, or seas are mentioned in your reading. Note that the same location may have different names in different times, including our own times. Rabbath Ammon in the Hebrew Scripture became Philadelphia in Revelation and is now Amman, Jordan.

Befriend the text.

Read with a pen or pencil or highlighter in hand and underline passages of interest. Look up unfamiliar words in a dictionary. Write notes in the margins when necessary. Some versions come with especially large margins just for this purpose. Thomas Cranmer probably had something else in mind, but he did say that we should "Read, *mark*, learn, and inwardly digest" the Scripture. This is still a good way to note things that strike you.

Practice reading the text out loud.

HOW TO READ THE ENTIRE BIBLE IN ONE YEAR

Reading the entire Bible is a formidable task and can frustrate even the most patient believer when approached willy-nilly. A measured and consistent walk through the Bible, however, can be done without tremendous fuss.

Consider purchasing a good "One Year" Bible.

Many good translations are published in special one-year editions. You may not want to make this your only Bible, but for reading in one year it can make the job much easier. It should combine daily Old and New Testament readings with a psalm or section from Proverbs. You might also consider Marek Zabriskie's popular Bible Challenge. It is available in electronic as well as print versions.

Choose a method that matches your personality and reading habits.

- You might choose to start with one book and skip around for the next. Begin with one of the four Gospels, such as John, then read an Old Testament book, like Genesis. Jump to one of the epistles, such as Ephesians. Skipping around may keep your attention fresh. Mark which ones you have read in the Table of Contents.
- Start with the first page and read straight through to the last. Keep in mind the first ten books of the Bible can get heavy and dry. Plowing through them may wear you out fast. Take a break with the Psalms or the Book of Job.

Covenant with a reading buddy or group.

Commit to each other that you will do your daily readings aloud together when possible and that you'll keep up with them when it's not.

When attempting to read the entire Bible in one year,
avoid reading late at night, as this will promote an unwelcome
association between God's word and drowsiness.

Celebrate your completed reading of the Bible.

At the end of your Year of the Bible, consider holding a ritual in
which you thank God for the experience.

Be Aware

- You do not earn your salvation by reading the Bible, but you
  may experience growth and deepening in your faith. Allow
  the Scriptures to speak to you. It is not for nothing that Jesus
  used the image of a seed planted in different kinds of soil to
  portray how the Word of God works.

- Many translations include a suggested one-year reading schedule broken into daily chunks.

- A good bookmark can be almost as important to daily reading as the reading itself. Find one you look forward to seeing each day when you open the book. Some Bibles come with ribbons built in!

- Avoid trying to read as much as you can each sitting. Set limits for yourself.

- Avoid reading late at night. Dozing off in the middle of the histories guarantees a later reread.

WHY EPISCOPALIANS HAVE THEIR OWN VERSION OF THE PSALMS

The Episcopal Church takes worship very seriously, and it's no surprise that singing plays a very important role. And not just hymn singing, but the singing of the Psalms as well. That's why the Book of Common Prayer contains a custom translation of the Psalms called "The Psalter." It is designed for singing and chanting the Bible's greatest songs in congregational worship.

Of course, Episcopalians did not invent the Psalter. The Hebrews sang the Psalms long before Jesus walked the earth, and there have been several translations down through the ages. However, the unique style and expertise the English brought to the Psalms have made the Psalter an important contribution to Christian literature, along with the Authorized Version (the "King James Bible") and the rest of the Book of Common Prayer.

Episcopalians are also the proud inheritors and practitioners of a unique style of singing the Psalms called "Anglican chant." This is the incredibly rich and even breathtaking style often sung by choirs in English cathedrals and many parish churches. It continues to enrich the worship of countless congregations. More than likely, your local Episcopal parish worships in this style during some portion of the year. (To find a parish near you, go to *theredbook.org*.)

The translation in the 1979 Book of Common Prayer was a new version of the Psalter, a departure from the 1549 and subsequent books (where the Psalter was the work of Myles Coverdale). Undertaking the revision of a text in constant use for over 400 years was a daunting task, and poets such as W.H. Auden were involved, in order both to preserve the dignity and cadence of the earlier text, and to ensure that the new version would flow well on modern tongues.

THE TOP TEN BIBLE HEROES

The Bible is filled with typical examples of heroism, but another kind of hero inhabits the pages of the Bible—those people who, against all odds, follow God no matter the outcome. These are heroes of faith.

Noah

Noah trusted God when God chose him to build an ark to save a remnant of humanity from destruction. Noah's trust became part of a covenant with God.

Abraham and Sarah

In extreme old age, Abraham and Sarah answered God's call to leave their home and travel to a strange land, where they became the parents of God's people.

Moses

Moses challenged the Egyptian powers to deliver God's people from bondage. He led a rebellious and contrary people for 40 years through the wilderness and gave them God's law.

Ruth

Ruth was a Gentile (Moabite) who risked her future happiness out of loyalty to her Jewish mother-in-law, Naomi, vowing to stick with her through good times and bad. She became the great-grandmother of King David, and thus a part of the family tree of Jesus.

David

King David, the youngest member of his family, defeated great enemies, turning Israel into a world power. He wrote psalms, led armies, and confessed his sins (he was far from perfect!) to the Lord.

Mary and Joseph

They responded to God's call to be the parents of the Messiah, although the call came through a pregnancy that was not the result of their marriage.

The Canaanite Woman

Desperate for her daughter's health, the Canaanite woman challenged Jesus by claiming God's love for all people (Matthew 15:21–28). Because of this, Jesus praised her faith.

Simon Peter

He was a man quick to speak but slow to think. When confronted, Peter denied ever having known Jesus. But in the power of forgiveness, Peter became a leader in the early church, an apostle and missionary to Rome.

Saul/Paul

Originally an enemy and persecutor of Christians, Paul experienced a powerful vision of Jesus, repented, and became a missionary to a wider Gentile world.

Phoebe

A contemporary of Paul's, Phoebe is believed to have delivered the Letter to the Romans after traveling some 800 miles from Cenchreae near Corinth to Rome. A wealthy woman, she used her influence to travel, to protect other believers, and to host worship in her home.

Phoebe is believed to have delivered the book of Romans after traveling 800 miles.

THE TOP TEN BIBLE VILLAINS

Satan

The Evil One is known by many names in the Bible and appears many places, but the devil's purpose is always the same: to disrupt and confuse people so they turn from God and seek to become their own gods.

The Serpent

In Eden, the serpent succeeded in tempting Eve to eat from the tree of the knowledge of good and evil (Genesis 3:1–7). If it weren't for the serpent, we'd all still be walking around naked, eating fresh fruit, and living forever.

Pharaoh

The notorious Pharaoh from the book of Exodus (perhaps Ramesses II) enslaved the Israelites. Moses demanded he "Let my people go," but Pharaoh refused. Ten plagues later, Pharaoh relented, then changed his mind again. In the end, with his army at the bottom of the sea, Pharaoh finally gave his slaves up to the wilderness.

Goliath

"The Philistine of Gath" stood six cubits in height (about nine feet tall) and, after challenging the Israelite army, thought young David was a pushover. David drilled Goliath in the head with a rock from his sling and gave God the glory (1 Samuel 17).

Jezebel

King Ahab of Israel's wife and a follower of Baal, Jezebel led her husband away from God and tried to kill off the prophets of the Lord. Elijah the prophet, however, was on the scene. He shamed Jezebel's false prophets and killed them (1 Kings 18:40). She later was killed as part of a coup.

one cubit

Goliath   David

*Though physically powerful, Goliath lost his battle
with young David, one of the Top 10 heroes of the Bible.*

Herod the Great

Afraid of any potential threat to his power, upon hearing about
the birth of the Messiah in Bethlehem, Herod asked the Magi to
pinpoint his location. Warned in a dream, they went home by
a different route and avoided Herod. In a rage, he ordered the
murder of every boy two years of age or younger in the vicinity of
Bethlehem. The baby Messiah escaped with his parents to Egypt
(Matthew 2:14–15).

Caiaphas

Caiaphas was a primary mover in organizing the plot against
Jesus, saying that it was better for one man to die than for the
whole people to suffer (John 11:50). This went against the

teaching of Rabbi Hillel that "whoever saves a single life, it is as if he has saved a whole world."

Judas Iscariot

One of Jesus' disciples, Judas earned 30 pieces of silver by betraying him to the authorities. He accomplished this by leading the soldiers into the garden of Gethsemane where he revealed Jesus with a kiss (Matthew 26–27).

Pontius Pilate

The consummate politician, the Roman governor chose to preserve his own status by giving the people what they wanted: Jesus' crucifixion. He washed his hands to signify self-absolution, but bloodied them instead.

God's People

We whine, we sin, we turn our backs on God over and over again. When given freedom, we blow it. When preached repentance by God's prophets, we stone them. When offered a Savior, we kill him. In the end, it must be admitted, God's people—us!—don't really shine. Only by God's grace and the gift of faith do we have hope.

FOUR REBELLIOUS THINGS JESUS DID

The prophet returned to his hometown (Luke 4:14–27).
Jesus returned to Nazareth, where he was raised, and was invited to read Scripture and preach. First, he insisted that the Scriptures he read were not just comforting promises of a distant future, but that they were being made real then and there. Second, he insisted God would bless foreigners with those same promises. This amounted to a rejection of ethnic superiority.

The rebel took a stand in the face of the authorities (John 11:55–12:11).
Jesus had become a problem, hunted by the religious authorities who wanted to kill him. Mary, Martha, and Lazarus threw a thank-you party for Jesus in Bethany, right outside Jerusalem, the authorities' stronghold. In spite of the threats to his life, Jesus went to the party. This was not just rebellion but a demonstration of how much Jesus loved his friends.

The king rode a royal procession right under Caesar's nose (Matthew 21:1–17, Mark 11:1–10, Luke 19:28–38, John 12:12–19).
Jesus entered Jerusalem during a great festival, in full view of adoring crowds, as a king come home to rule. Riding a donkey (and a colt, according to Matthew), heralded by the people with cloaks and branches, accompanied by the royal anthem (Psalm 118), he rode in to claim Jerusalem for God and himself as God's anointed. The Roman overlords and the religious leaders watched this seditious act and prepared for a crucifixion.

The rabbi broke with tradition and angered the other religious leaders (Matthew 12:1–8, Mark 7:1–15, 11:15–18).
Jesus was in many ways a typical rabbi of his era, but his teaching often conflicted with the most popular interpretations of his time. His teachings on the Sabbath, the purity laws, and the Temple were controversial and led to resentment and opposition.

FIVE UNPOPULAR PROPHETS

New Testament tax collectors weren't alone in being hated. Here are five notable bearers of God's message and what made them so unpopular.

Amos

Amos gained few friends when he told the Israelites that their privilege came with responsibility. He prophesied against Israel's enemies but then challenged Israel's practices as worse than those of the nations they hated. He even said that Israel would be destroyed. Amos let God's people know that God hates violence and oppression of the weak—no matter who's doing it.

The Lord's prophets tended to be unpopular, especially among the wealthy, because their messages called for justice toward others and fidelity toward God. Amos was particularly unpopular for this reason.

Nahum

Nahum told the people of Nineveh that even a mighty army wouldn't keep a nation safe from God's judgment. About 150 years earlier, Jonah had told them to repent (and they did), but they quickly returned to old ways. God gave Nahum a new message of destruction for them, but they weren't scared because they had a strong army. So while the city was falling, Nahum ridiculed them by suggesting they draw water (in the midst of a flood), and add bricks to the already demolished city wall.

Micah

Micah told the people that God wants disciples to have humble hearts and behave with justice and mercy. He said God would come and destroy the nation because the powerful had schemed to steal from the poor and followed false prophets. They thought following ritual was enough. It wasn't.

Zephaniah

Zephaniah was another prophet in Judah. He made enemies by warning that even those who refused to worship idols would face God's judgment because they didn't follow God.

Jeremiah

God called Jeremiah to be a prophet when he was just a boy. This gave him more time to confront God's people about their self-focused lives. He was persecuted bitterly by Judah's last two kings—and even his own extended family tried to kill him. Jeremiah's messages were many—but this one still speaks: Those who are godly may suffer persecution, but they should look to God for salvation!

FIVE INSPIRING WOMEN IN THE BIBLE

There are more than 300 women mentioned in the Bible. Some have names recorded, others are referred to as "the women" or some other designation the defines them in terms of their relationship to someone else (usually a man, as in the case of Simon Peter's "mother-in-law" [Luke 4:38]). Theologians and scholars have begun to highlight the lives of these many women and speak of their contributions to the story of God. Here are a few of the more inspiring examples (and we have the names of all but one).

Miriam, Jochabed, Puah, Shiprah, and "Pharaoh's Daughter"

These five women were instrumental in the survival of Moses. Without their quick thinking, strong courage, and love of God, Moses would have drowned in the Nile River along with many other baby boys. *Note: We are naming more than one woman in this instance, but that's fine. Salvation is sometimes a team effort.*

Rahab

Rahab was a prostitute who lived at the outskirts of Jericho. She concealed the spies that Joshua sent to scope out the city (Joshua 2:1–21, 6:17–25). In return for that she not only was spared, but became an example of faith even mentioned in the Christian Scriptures (Hebrews 11:31 and James 2:25).

Esther

When an evil politician threatened to annihilate her people, Queen Esther used her beauty and skills in negotiation to save them. Esther is commemorated each year during Purim, a Jewish holiday celebrating deliverance and the plans for extermination that backfired.

Lydia was a "God fearer," someone who received the gospel of Jesus Christ and was used to spread the good news in her town.

Lydia

Lydia was known as a worshiper of God who regularly prayed with her household. She became a Christian and began a house church and attended to the needs of the apostle Paul.

Mary, the Mother of the Lord

At a young age, Mary answered a resounding "Yes" to the angel's request that she bear God's Son. She did this at considerable risk, because under the Law she could have been charged with adultery when found to be pregnant by someone other than her husband-to-be.

THE TOP TEN BIBLE MIRACLES AND WHAT THEY MEAN

Creation

God created the universe and everything that is in it, and God continues to create and recreate without ceasing. God's first and ongoing miracle was *to reveal that the creation has a purpose.*

The Passover

The Israelites were enslaved by Pharaoh, a ruler who believed the people belonged to him, not to God. In the last of ten plagues, God visited the houses of all the Egyptians to kill the firstborn male in each one. *God alone is Lord of the people, and no human can claim ultimate power over another human being.*

The Exodus

God's people were fleeing Egypt when Pharaoh dispatched his army to force them back into slavery. The army trapped the people with their backs to a sea, but God parted the water and the Israelites walked across to freedom while Pharaoh's troops and chariots were destroyed. *God chose to free us from all forms of tyranny so we may use that freedom to serve God and each other.*

Manna

After the people crossed the sea to freedom, they complained that they were going to starve to death. They even asked to go back to Egypt. God sent manna from the skies, so the people lived. *God cares for us even when we give up, pine for our slavery, and lose faith. God never abandons us. Bread is not the only or principal source of life.*

The Incarnation

The immortal and infinite God became a human being, choosing to be born of a woman. *God loved us enough to become one of us in Jesus of Nazareth, forever bridging the divide that had separated us from God.*

Jesus healed the paralyzed man

People carried a paralyzed friend to Jesus. Jesus said, "Your sins are forgiven" (Mark 2:5). *This means that Jesus has the power to forgive our sins—and he does so as a free gift.*

Jesus calmed the storm

Jesus was asleep in a boat with his disciples when a great storm came up and threatened to sink it. He said, "Peace! Be still!" (Mark 4:39). Then the storm immediately calmed. *Jesus is Lord over even the powers of nature.*

The Resurrection

Human beings executed Jesus, but God raised him from the dead on the third day. *Through baptism, we share in Jesus' death, so we will also share in eternal life with God the Father, Son, and Holy Spirit. Christ conquered death.*

Pentecost

Jesus ascended into heaven, but he did not leave the church powerless or alone. On the fiftieth day after the Passover (Pentecost means "fiftieth"), the Holy Spirit descended on the apostles to create the church. *The Holy Spirit is present with us always.*

The Baptism of Cornelius

Saint Peter had a dreamlike vision that he came to understand as meaning no people were beyond God's care. He went to preach to the Roman Cornelius, and as he did, the Holy Spirit descended again, just as at Pentecost. *This opened the way for salvation to extend to the Gentile world—which includes most of us!*

JESUS' TWELVE APOSTLES (PLUS MATTHIAS AND PAUL)

While Jesus had many disciples (students and followers), the Bible focuses particularly on the twelve who were closest to him. Tradition says that of these, eleven spread Jesus' message throughout the known world (Matthew 28:18–20). (You know which one didn't!) For this reason, they were known as apostles, a word that means "sent ones."

Andrew

A fisherman and the first disciple to follow Jesus, Andrew brought his brother, Simon Peter, to Jesus.

Bartholomew

Also called Nathanael, tradition has it that he was martyred by being skinned alive.

James, son of Zebedee

James, with John and Peter, was one of Jesus' closest disciples. Herod Agrippa killed James because of his faith, which made him a martyr (Acts 12:2).

His brother, John

John (or one of his followers) is thought to be the author of the Gospel of John and three letters of John. He probably died of natural causes in old age.

Matthew

Matthew was a tax collector and, therefore, probably an outcast even among his own people. He is attributed with the authorship of the Gospel of Matthew.

Peter

Peter was a fisherman who was brought to faith by his brother Andrew. The tradition is that he was martyred in Rome by being crucified upside down.

Philip

Philip, possibly a Greek, is responsible for bringing Bartholomew (Nathanael) to faith. He is thought to have died in a city called Phrygia.

James the Less

James was called "the Less" so he wouldn't be confused with James, the brother of John, or James, Jesus' brother.

Simon

Simon is often called "the Zealot." Zealots were a political group in Jesus' day that favored the forceful overthrow of the Roman government.

Jude

Jude may have worked with Simon the Zealot in Persia (Iran) where they were martyred on the same day.

Thomas

"Doubting" Thomas is thought to have preached the message of Jesus in India.

Judas Iscariot

Judas was the treasurer for Jesus' disciples and the one who betrayed Jesus for 30 pieces of silver. He killed himself for his betrayal.

Matthias

Matthias was chosen by lot to replace Judas. It is thought that he worked mostly in Ethiopia.

Paul

Paul traveled widely and is considered responsible for bringing the Gospel to many. He wrote many letters to believers, which are included in the New Testament.

THE FIVE BIGGEST MISCONCEPTIONS ABOUT THE BIBLE

The Bible was written in a short period of time.

Christians believe that God inspired the Bible writers, over many centuries. God inspired people to write down important histories, laws, traditions, songs, wise sayings, poetry, visions, dreams, and prophetic words. All told, the entire Bible formed over a period spanning anywhere from 800 to 1,400 years!

One person wrote the Bible.

Many of the Bible's books do not indicate who the author is. Some give a traditional designation, but often the same book shows clear signs of many hands and significant editing. For instance, there are two creation accounts and two accounts of the flood woven together in Genesis, and likely more than Moses were involved. Much of Scripture does not identify the human hand behind it, and some parts of the Bible, such as the Song of Deborah, can be credited to women as well as men.

The entire Bible is to be taken literally.

While many parts of the Bible are meant as descriptions of historical events, other parts are intended as illustrations of God's truth, such as the Song of Solomon, the Book of Revelation, and Jesus' parable of the good Samaritan. So when Jesus says, "If your right eye causes you to sin, tear it out and throw it away" (Matthew 5:29), please do not take the saying literally!

People in Bible times were unenlightened.

During the centuries in which the Bible was written, some of history's greatest thinkers lived and worked. Many of these philosophers, architects, mathematicians, orators, theologians, historians, doctors, military tacticians, inventors, engineers, poets, and play-wrights are still quoted today and their works are still in use.

The Bible is a single book.

The Bible is actually a collection of books, letters, and other writings—more like a library than a book. There are 39 books in the Hebrew Scriptures, what Christians call the "Old" Testament, and 27 books (mostly letters) in the New Testament. There are up to 18 "deuterocanonical" books, sometimes called "the Apocrypha," depending on which tradition is followed.

DO EPISCOPALIANS BELIEVE IN EVOLUTION?

Some do and some don't. However, most of us believe in thoughtful dialogue regarding the role of science in religion. The 2006 General Convention affirmed "that God is Creator, in accordance with the witness of Scripture and the ancient Creeds of the Church; that the theory of evolution provides a fruitful and unifying scientific explanation for the emergence of life on earth; that many theological interpretations of origins can readily embrace an evolutionary outlook; and that an acceptance of evolution is entirely compatible with an authentic and living Christian faith" (Resolution A129).

Many Episcopalians hold to the idea that science and religion are not opposed to one another, but rather are complementary. They both tell us important things about different aspects of reality. They both share the noble mission of discovering truth. In simplistic terms it might be said that science labors to tell us "how," while it is the job of religion to address "why."

Episcopalians find the "because" in response to "why?" in the Bible. That is not to say we are Bible literalists; most of us are not. However, it is to say that we hold to the belief found in the Book of Common Prayer that the Bible "contains all things necessary to salvation" (BCP 868). That is also to say that the Bible doesn't contain all necessary truths about everything else. The Bible was not written as a science textbook, nor do we believe it should be used as one. Most of us believe the mystery and complexity of the universe reveals a mysterious and complex God, and we have much to learn about both the universe and God.

This means that most Episcopalians tend to be rather curious about the world and how it works. Many of us welcome new scientific discoveries, not because we're being contrary, but because we believe they can shed light on our understandings of God's world and, therefore, God.

DOES THE BIBLE CONDEMN GAY PEOPLE?

No more than the Bible condemns straight people.

At issue here is a big question that continues to challenge many religious people in America—and not just in the Episcopal Church. Some Christians believe the Bible's clear, literal interpretation leaves no room for salvation for lesbian, gay, bisexual, and transgender ("LGBT") people. Other Christians, including many Episcopalians, not only read these texts differently, but look to science, reason, and experience as part of the conversation and come to a different conclusion.

As with nuclear warfare and stem cell research, there are certain issues that exist today that were not notable at the time of Jesus. Committed, responsible, adult same-gender relationships are one example. (While same-sex relationships existed, in the Graeco-Roman culture, they usually were temporary and involved an age or class difference, rather than being permanent unions of two adult partners.) It's true both that Jesus never talked about homosexuality, and that some texts that appear to mention it are negative—but they also leave plenty of room for interpretation. If, as many scholars accept, these texts were addressing the kind of same-sex relationships prevalent in Graeco-Roman times (pederasty, prostitution, abuse of slaves, and orgies linked with pagan worship), then they may have little application to permanent, faithful, and monogamous same-sex relationships between adult Christians. As with many Christians, Episcopalians read these verses keeping the historical context in mind, and the way these texts fit in with the larger message of the Bible.

This larger message leads many of us to concentrate on issues like world hunger, desperate poverty, injustice, violence, and war. Jesus calls us all to lead holy lives no matter what our sexual orientation. But holy lives—including the loving relationships we form—are defined by much more than sex and gender. The Bible defines them with words like love, joy, peace, patience, generosity, goodness, kindness, and self-control (Galatians 5:22).

Yes, the Bible condemns all who have sinned and fallen short of God's glory. But the Bible also tells us that Jesus redeems all who call upon his name. Episcopalians believe this redemption is open to everybody. As the apostle Paul once put it, "There is no longer Jew or Greek, there is no longer slave or free, there is no longer male and female; for all of you are one in Christ Jesus" (Galatians 3:28).

The Episcopal Church has wrestled with the issue of the place of LGBT people in the church, and has moved over the decades since the 1970s from toleration to affirmation—not of sexuality, but of the moral values of fidelity, commitment, and love.

MAPS, CHARTS,
AND DIAGRAMS

THE EXODUS

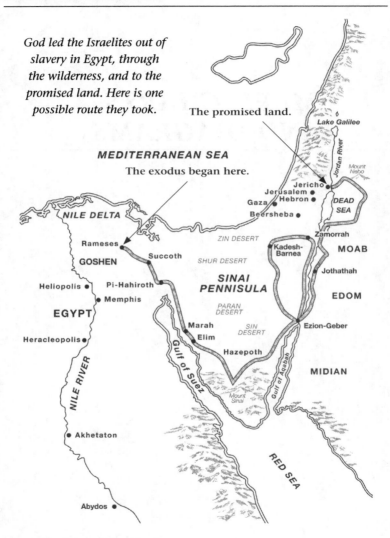

God led the Israelites out of slavery in Egypt, through the wilderness, and to the promised land. Here is one possible route they took.

The promised land.

MEDITERRANEAN SEA

The exodus began here.

Lake Galilee

Jordan River

Mount Nebo

Jericho

Jerusalem ● Hebron ●

Gaza ●

Beersheba ●

DEAD SEA

NILE DELTA

Rameses ●

GOSHEN

Succoth ●

ZIN DESERT

Zamorrah ●

SHUR DESERT

Kadesh-Barnea ●

MOAB

Heliopolis ●

Pi-Hahiroth ●

● Memphis

SINAI PENNISULA

Jothathah ●

EDOM

EGYPT

PARAN DESERT

Marah ●

Elim ●

SIN DESERT

Ezion-Geber ●

Heracleopolis ●

Hazepoth ●

Gulf of Suez

Gulf of Aqabah

MIDIAN

Mount Sinai

● Akhetaton

RED SEA

NILE RIVER

Abydos ●

THE ARK OF THE COVENANT

God told the Israelites to place the stone tablets—the "covenant"—of the law into the Ark of the Covenant. The Israelites believed that God was invisibly enthroned above the vessel and went before them wherever they traveled.

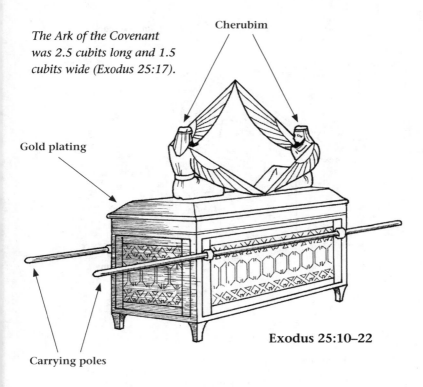

Cherubim

The Ark of the Covenant was 2.5 cubits long and 1.5 cubits wide (Exodus 25:17).

Gold plating

Carrying poles

Exodus 25:10–22

JERUSALEM IN JESUS' TIME

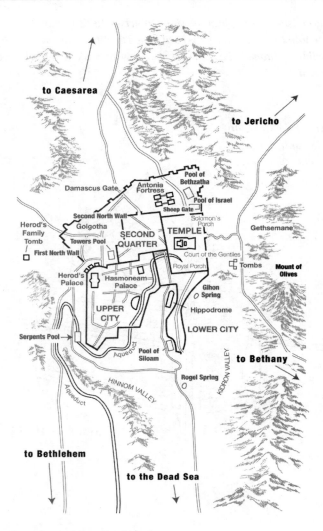

to Caesarea

to Jericho

Pool of Bethzatha

Damascus Gate

Antonia Fortress

Pool of Israel

Second North Wall

Sheep Gate

Solomon's Porch

Herod's Family Tomb

Golgotha

Gethsemane

Towers Pool

SECOND QUARTER

TEMPLE

First North Wall

Court of the Gentiles

Royal Porch

Tombs

Mount of Olives

Herod's Palace

Hasmonean Palace

Gihon Spring

UPPER CITY

Hippodrome

LOWER CITY

Serpents Pool

Aqueduct

Pool of Siloam

to Bethany

Rogel Spring

KIDRON VALLEY

HINNOM VALLEY

Aqueduct

to Bethlehem

to the Dead Sea

THE PASSION
AND CRUCIFIXION

Judas betrayed Jesus with a kiss, saying,
"The one I will kiss is the man; arrest him" (Matthew 26:48).

Peter denied Jesus three times (Matthew 26:69–75).

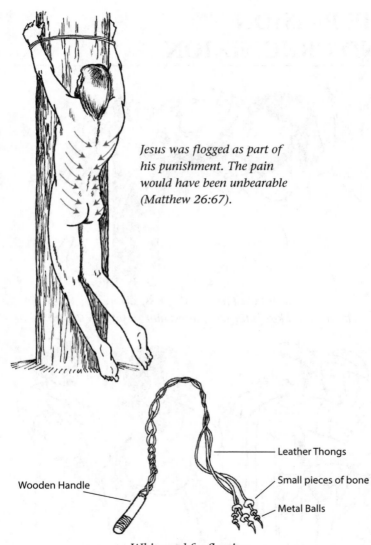

Jesus was flogged as part of his punishment. The pain would have been unbearable (Matthew 26:67).

Wooden Handle

Leather Thongs

Small pieces of bone

Metal Balls

Whip used for flogging

*After being flogged, carrying the patibulum
was nearly impossible for Jesus.*

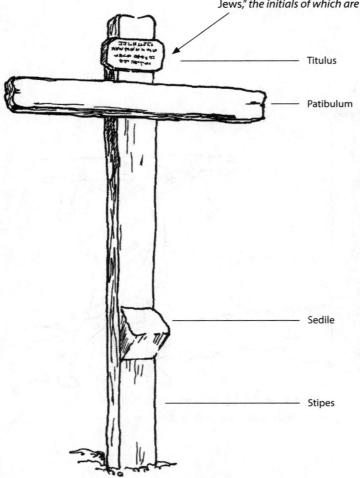

The charge against Jesus said, "*Jesus of Nazareth*, the king of the Jews," the initials of which are I.N.R.I.

Titulus

Patibulum

Sedile

Stipes

Crucifixion was so common in Jesus' time that the Romans had special names for the parts of the cross.

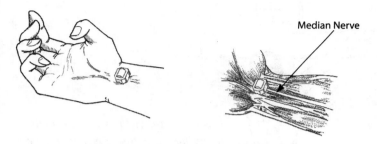

Typical crucifixion involved being nailed to the cross through the wrists—an excruciatingly painful punishment.

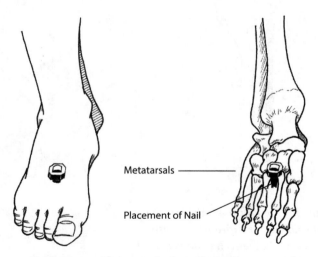

During a crucifixion, a single nail usually was used to pin both feet together to the cross.

Eventually, the victim would be unable to lift himself to take a breath, and he would suffocate.

While the Romans broke the legs of the men who were crucified next to Jesus, they found that Jesus had already died. To make sure, they pierced his side with a spear, probably to puncture his heart (John 19:34).

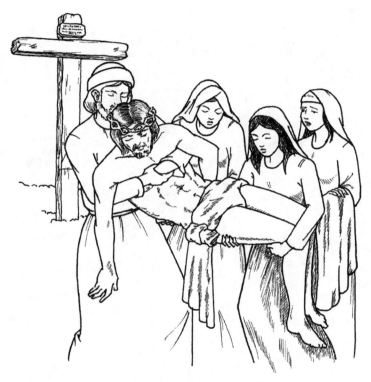

Joseph of Arimathea and several women took Jesus down and carried him to the tomb (Matthew 27:57–61).

The miracle of resurrection took place three days later when Jesus was raised from the dead.

FAMILY TREE OF CHRISTIANITY

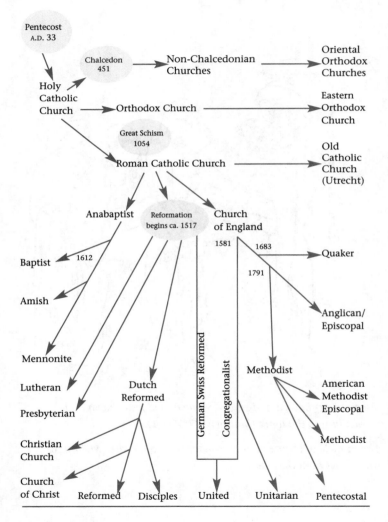

ANGLICAN STUFF
AND GLOSSARY

WHERE ANGLICANISM STANDS
IN THE RELIGION OF THE WORLD
AND WITHIN CHRISTIANITY

Ever since prehistoric times humans have felt the hairs rise on the backs of their necks when encountering what Rudolph Otto called "the fascinating and tremendous mystery" that leads them to believe there is more to the world than just . . . well, the world. It is more than we can bite off and chew here to outline the whole history of world religion, so what follows is a brief sketch. It is intended to give a general idea of where Christianity fits in, and how Anglicanism relates to the larger Christian world.

Some cultures preserve something of that prehistoric feeling of awe and imagine the world itself, or different aspects of it or objects in it, to be *animated* (that is, having a soul or souls). Individual events or objects or actions could become charged with spiritual power, for good or bad. Often these souls or spirits came to be identified as gods, sometimes with particular worldly areas of responsibility. If you think of what we call Greek mythology, which for many (yes, they had atheists, too!) was religious belief, you may recall Zeus' thunderbolts or Poseidon's trident. The people of Scandinavia and Egypt had religious systems with similar assignments, as did many of the cultures of Asia.

Often these arrays of deities had a ranking in which one or a few deities were considered superior to all the rest. Many Greeks and Romans came to consider Zeus (or Jove or Jupiter) as the principle god, and similar movements took place in Asia and Egypt. There are even traces of this kind of shift in the Bible, such as the song in Exodus 15:11 (also part of Psalm 86), "Who is like you, O God, among the gods?"

Ultimately the faith of those who would come to form the people of Israel took a turn toward belief in a single God, denying the existence of any other deities (though continuing to recognize the existence of other spiritual beings, as angels or demons, but not gods). A different path was taken in Asia when Buddhism came to challenge the notion that there is any god, or God, at all. So while Judaism moved into monotheism, Buddhism came to represent a form of non-theistic religion.

The New Testament records, in the Gospels, Epistles, and Acts especially, the emergence of Christianity—first as a movement within Judaism (as one of many, since Judaism in the first century was rich with different schools of thought, some of them quite negative toward each other). Eventually, in part due to the increased outreach to Gentiles, Christianity came to be distinguished, and ultimately to distinguish itself, from Judaism, while still considering that faith to be part of its heritage. This led to many hurtful and harmful reactions through the centuries, some of them recent enough to be enshrined in living memory—and may we never forget!

The seventh century CE saw the emergence of Islam, described by Muhammad as a revelation of the timeless truth about the One God through many prophets, including Abraham, Moses and Jesus, culminating in his own prophecy. The tensions between Islam and Christianity form a major part of Middle Eastern, African, and European history. On the Indian subcontinent, similar tensions between Islam and Hinduism were and are also important to this day.

Meanwhile, Christianity itself had been changing. Even the Epistles of Paul testify to disagreements and sectarianism within the first-century church. Although there was a mainstream church that sought to preserve the faith of the apostles, there were sidestreams of Christian belief that came to be labeled as heresies (from the Greek word for "parties"). Much of the division and dissension centered on how people understood the One God as Trinity, and the divine and human natures united in the one person of Christ. These disagreements were addressed, and agreed-upon statements were hammered out in a series of councils of church leaders from 325 CE on. The first major split (that is, apart from those side-stream heresies, some of which continued to maintain considerable influence) came when a number of Christian leaders rejected the decisions of the Council of Chalcedon held in 451. This included the churches in Armenia, Egypt, and Ethiopia, today referred to as the Oriental Orthodox churches (to be distinguished from the Eastern Orthodox churches).

The second major split came in 1054, in what is known as the "Great Schism." This formalized a long-standing tension between the Roman Catholic and Eastern Orthodox churches. Many factors played a part in this division, some theological, but some concerning authority and culture. The fifteenth and sixteenth centuries brought more divisions, mostly in Europe, due to the Anabaptist and Reformation movements, which had influence on England as well. These divisions and revolts against church authority centered in Rome often involved theological differences, especially concerning the sacraments of Baptism and Eucharist, and the nature of clerical leadership, whether by bishops or elders, or by the whole community of the faithful. Politics also played a part, of course, particularly in England, where Henry VIII was considered a loyal Roman Catholic (for his defense of Roman doctrine against Luther) until his personal circumstances led to a breach with the papacy.

This led to the independence of the Church of England, but little changed in terms of worship and doctrine as long as Henry was still in charge. The separation did open a window for many English church leaders to press the case for reform, and over the years from Henry's death to the reign of Elizabeth I, the structures and beliefs of Anglicanism took form. It is perhaps interesting to note that some of the revolutionary changes made by Anglicans and other churches of the Reformation, such as the use of the local language in worship, and sharing the Cup in Communion, have since been adopted even by the Roman Catholic Church from which the others split.

So what distinguishes Anglicans from Roman Catholics and other Christians? The old saying, "Just like Rome without the pope," is right about "the pope." Anglican churches throughout the world, starting with the Church of England, rejected the idea that the whole church should be governed globally from a single hub by a single person. The idea of "the national church" emerged; and to this day the various member bodies of the Anglican Communion do not form a single world-church but a fellowship of churches with no central governing body or single leader. The Archbishop of Canterbury is accorded a role as a respected convener of meetings, but has no authority outside his own Church of England. This means that different parts of the Anglican Communion, in spite of their common heritage, may have strong differences of opinion, as has been the case in recent years concerning the ordination of women, and the place of LGBT people in the church.

Each Anglican church has its own governing structure, usually with a principal bishop (the primate, president, or presiding bishop) and consisting of numerous dioceses—geographical areas with their own bishops, divided into parishes in which priests and deacons lead and serve congregations. Neither the parishes nor the dioceses are completely independent. To take the Episcopal Church as an example: Parishes are governed by the canons (church laws) of the diocese, and with the dioceses by the Constitution and Canons of the whole Episcopal Church. In most dioceses, lay representatives of the parishes and clergy form the diocesan convention, and the bishops, together with lay and clergy deputies from each diocese, form the General Convention. (See the next article.)

One of the features that distinguishes Anglicans both from Roman Catholics and some Protestant traditions also has to do with authority, particularly in the case of doctrine. Anglicans hold fast to some core doctrines, but readily admit that not only *can* the church get things wrong, but that it *has*! This leads to a kind of *humility* and *provisionality* to all but the most formal, and biblically based, theological positions, such as those in the Nicene Creed.

How Anglicans regard Scripture as a source of authority also separates us from some of the Protestant bodies that adopt a "Bible alone" (*sola scriptura*) approach. Anglicans don't hold the Bible to be either our only source or one that is in all things perfectly clear. The helpful phrase from our Anglican forebears is that the Scripture is *sufficient*—that it tells what we need to know for salvation through Christ, and that nothing can be required as an article of belief if it cannot be found clearly stated in Scripture. And since Scripture is often not clear (in contradiction to those churches who declare it always is, in their term *perspicacious*), it must be understood and interpreted by human beings who, being fallible (see above), sometimes get it wrong. (By the way, Anglicans read the Apocrypha or Deuterocanonical books as part of liturgy and for instruction, unlike many Protestants who don't include them at all, but aren't supposed to rely on them to make doctrinal points, unlike the Roman Catholics.)

Another feature of Anglicanism concerns the belief that the forms of worship do not need to be the same everywhere, and that local customs can be respected. This led originally to the creation of the Book of Common Prayer in England, and has led to its continued revision in most of the Anglican Communion. Just the idea of having a "set liturgy" distinguishes Anglicans from the non-liturgical churches such as those of the Baptist and Pentecostal traditions, whose worship services are much more at the discretion of their leaders and members.

Anglicans also part from many of the Protestant bodies in the view of ordained ministry, retaining three "orders" of deacon, priest, and bishop. Some Protestant churches do not have the order of deacon, and some lack bishops, but Anglicans maintain all three as part of our full ministry. Moreover, we hold that our bishops are part of a "historic episcopate" (sometimes called "the apostolic succession") going back to the earliest days of the church. Perhaps most importantly, lay people also play a considerable role in the government, leadership, ministry, and mission of the church, and in the Episcopal Church play a major role in the selection of ordained leaders, as well as the governance of the church from the parish up through the General Convention.

This short essay has touched on just a few of the main things that distinguish Episcopalians from other Christians. There are, of course, many other beliefs and practices we share with some and not with others: infant as well as adult baptism, a sacramental understanding of the presence of Christ in the Holy Eucharist, the availability of (without insistence upon) private confession, and the openness of ordination to women.

WHAT IS GENERAL CONVENTION?

Since 1789 the General Convention has been the central governing body of the Episcopal Church. It consists of a House of Deputies (lay people and clergy chosen by their dioceses) and the House of Bishops (consisting of all bishops, both active and retired, though not all attend all meetings). The General Convention meets every three years. Its primary responsibility is the maintenance of the Constitution and Canons of the church, its governing documents, which are subject to amendment at each session. (Changes to the Constitution and the Book of Common Prayer require the agreement of two consecutive sessions.)

In addition to such amendments to church law and liturgy, the General Convention will normally consider some hundreds of additional resolutions concerning national and world affairs, interreligious and ecumenical relations, and social issues, among other topics. All resolutions are assigned to legislative committees made up of bishops and deputies. They hold open hearings and make recommendations to the House that first votes on each resolution. Because the two Houses meet and deliberate separately, all actions must be agreed to by both (in identical language) in order to become law or policy, so if a resolution fails in the House of initial action, it never makes it to the other.

Between sessions of the General Convention, the Executive Council, a number of interim committees and commissions, and the staff of the Presiding Bishop work to put the decisions made into effect, and offer proposals for consideration at the next session of the Convention.

The sessions take place in different cities every three years, and are open to visitors. You might consider dropping in to a session of the General Convention when it takes place in a city near you.

PROVINCES OF THE ANGLICAN COMMUNION

- The Anglican Church in Aotearoa, New Zealand, and Polynesia
- The Anglican Church of Australia
- The Church of Bangladesh
- Igreja Episcopal Anglicana do Brasil
- The Anglican Church of Burundi
- The Anglican Church of Canada
- The Church of the Province of Central Africa
- Iglesia Anglicana de la Region Central de America
- Province de L'Eglise Anglicane Du Congo
- The Church of England
- Hong Kong Sheng Kung Hui
- The Church of the Province of the Indian Ocean
- The Church of Ireland
- The Nippon Sei Ko Kai (The Anglican Communion in Japan)
- The Episcopal Church in Jerusalem & the Middle East
- The Anglican Church of Kenya
- The Anglican Church of Korea
- The Church of the Province of Melanesia
- La Iglesia Anglicana de Mexico
- The Church of the Province of Myanmar (Burma)
- The Church of Nigeria
- The Church of North India (United)
- The Church of Pakistan (United)
- The Anglican Church of Papua New Guinea
- The Episcopal Church in the Philippines
- L'Eglise Episcopal au Rwanda

- The Scottish Episcopal Church
- Church of the Province of South East Asia
- The Church of South India (United)
- The Church of the Province of Southern Africa
- Iglesia Anglicana del Cono Sur de America
- The Episcopal Church of the Sudan
- The Anglican Church of Tanzania
- The Church of the Province of Uganda
- The Episcopal Church
- The Church in Wales
- The Church of the Province of West Africa
- The Church in the Province of the West Indies

The following are designated "Extra-Provincial," meaning they are not connected to a geographic province, as are other provinces of the Anglican Communion:

- The Church of Ceylon (Extra-Provincial to the Archbishop of Canterbury)
- Iglesia Episcopal de Cuba
- Bermuda (Extra-Provincial to the Archbishop of Canterbury)
- The Lusitanian Church (Extra-Provincial to the Archbishop of Canterbury)
- The Reformed Episcopal Church of Spain (Extra-Provincial to the Archbishop of Canterbury)
- Falkland Islands (Extra-Provincial to the Archbishop of Canterbury)

A Note on Internal Provinces

The Episcopal Church (and some other member churches of the Anglican Communion, such as the Church of England, the Anglican Church of Canada, and the Anglican Church of Australia, to name a few) also have *internal* "provinces." England has two

(Canterbury and York) and The Episcopal Church has nine, dividing up the "domestic dioceses" within the U.S. and including the overseas dioceses. The map on pages 96 and 97 shows the provinces, and they are described in the Canons in Title I Canon 9.

Other Churches in Communion with the Episcopal Church

The Episcopal Church is also in communion with and shares ministries with the Old Catholic Churches of the Union of Utrecht (who split from the Roman Catholic Church in the late nineteenth century), the Mar Thoma Syrian Church of Malabar, the Philippine Independent Church, the Evangelical Lutheran Church in America, and the Northern and Southern Provinces of the Moravian Church in America. Dialogues with many other churches continue with an eye toward mutual recognition and cooperation.

GLOSSARY OF EPISCOPAL TERMS

The following words aren't unique to the Episcopal Church, but you are likely to come across them. Many of these words involve worship, liturgy, or church architecture. Some of them have ordinary meanings in addition to *special* meanings they convey in a church context.

acolyte: From the Greek for "to follow"; a liturgical assistant (often but not necessarily a young person) who serves in such various roles as crucifer, torchbearer, banner-bearer, book-bearer, candle-lighter, and server.

Advent: From the Latin for "coming"; the four weeks before Christmas which constitute the first season of the liturgical year.

Advent wreath: A wreath with four (or five) candles, used during the four weeks of Advent (with the fifth candle lit at Christmas).

affusion: The most common form for baptism, in which water is poured over the head of the one being baptized.

Agnus Dei: An anthem said or sung just before the administration of Communion, beginning, "O Lamb of God."

alb: Full-length white vestment used in worship since the sixth century; usually worn with a rope cincture. Worn by presiding and assisting ministers, acolytes, and sometimes choristers.

alms: Financial contributions used for outreach to the needy or the suffering.

alms basonor basin: A shallow bowl, usually metal or wood, used to collect and present monetary offerings.

altar: Table in the chancel used for the celebration of the Holy Communion. It is the central furnishing of the sanctuary.

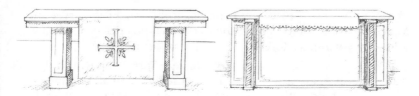

altar rail: Railing enclosing the chancel at which people stand or kneel to receive Holy Communion.

ambo: A pulpit, reading desk, or lectern from which Scripture is read and sometimes the Gospel preached.

Amen: From the Hebrew for "truly" or "so be it," it represents an affirmation at the end of a prayer.

antependium: Fabric decoration for the pulpit, lectern, or altar that "hangs in front" of it.

Apocrypha: Term used in some traditions to describe additional books of Scripture that were later not included in the Hebrew Bible, but formed a part of the second-century BCE Greek translation; called Deuterocanonical ("second canon") in the Roman Catholic tradition. Distinguished from the apocryphal books that are not included in any Bible.

apse: The semicircular (or polygonal) projection or alcove at the end of the chancel in traditional church architecture.

archbishop: A bishop who leads a province. The Episcopal Church does not use this term for its bishops.

archdeacon: A senior church leader (usually ordained, and often a priest) who exercises a role in a subdivision of a diocese or with a specific portfolio of tasks.

Ascension Day: Principal feast occurring 40 days after Easter Day, celebrating Christ's ascension into heaven.

ashes: Symbol of repentance and mortality used in the Ash Wednesday liturgy; made by burning palms from previous year.

Ash Wednesday: First day of Lent; occurs between February 4 and March 10. Name derives from the traditional practice of imposing ashes on worshipers' foreheads as a sign of penitence.

asperges, aspergillium, and aspersorium: Sprinkling with holy water, the sprinkler (sometimes a leafy branch or small bouquet, often a metal rod with a receptacle attached), and the vessel used to carry the blessed water.

assistant (priest): A priest who serves a parish at the selection and under the direction of the rector. Sometimes called a curate or associate.

assistant bishop: A bishop who serves under contract to a diocese other than the one to which elected originally, under the direction of the diocesan bishop.

assisting bishop: A bishop (usually having resigned from a previous jurisdiction, and often in retirement) who assists a diocese by performing some episcopal functions.

aumbry: (Sometimes spelled *ambry*) A small cupboard usually attached to a wall of the sanctuary, in which the holy oils may be kept.

baptism: The sacrament of water and the Holy Spirit, in which we are joined to Christ's death and resurrection and initiated into the church. Usually performed by affusion (pouring water over the head of one held or leaning over a font) or immersion (pouring water over one standing in the font, or lowered into it) rather than submersion (being completely lowered under the surface).

Baptismal Covenant: Statements of belief and promises made by baptizands and their sponsors, and the entire assembly, during the baptismal liturgy, and at times of the year as a renewal of those promises.

baptistery: The area in which the baptismal font is located; sometimes a separate chapel.

Benedictus: (benn-eh-DIK-tus) Latin title for the Gospel canticle "Blessed be the God of Israel," in Morning Prayer, from Luke

1:68–79. Also refers to "Blessed is he who comes in the name of the Lord," in the Eucharist.

blue: Liturgical color for Advent in some churches; symbolizes hope; sometimes used for feasts of the Virgin Mary.

boat: A small vessel, usually of metal, used to carry incense. Sometimes carried by a *boat bearer* to assist the thurifer.

Book of Common Prayer: Abbreviated BCP, this is the official worship formulary of Anglican churches; the version used in the Episcopal Church is based on the English edition of 1662, revised in 1785–1789 to include portions of the 1549 version; further revised in 1892, 1928, and 1979.

Book of Occasional Services: A collection of authorized rites supplemental to those in the Book of Common Prayer.

burse: Square fabric-covered case in which the communion linens are often carried to and from the altar.

candlelighter: Long-handled device used to light and extinguish candles.

candlestick: Ornamental base holder for candle.

canon: 1) The officially recognized content of the Bible, varying from church to church; 2) A church law; 3) A clerical title indicating a role in the governance of a cathedral, or on the staff of a bishop; sometimes honorary.

cassock: Full-length black garment worn as part of the clergy habit (and also by some acolytes and choristers). Bishops and deans of cathedrals sometimes wear a cassock in violet or purple.

catechumen: A person (usually an adult or older youth) preparing for Holy Baptism through a process of formation and special rites leading up to baptism, often at the Easter Vigil.

catechumenate: The process for preparing adults and older youth for Holy Baptism, often culminating at the Easter Vigil. It is a process of growth in spirituality, worship, service, as well as learning, and is based on the practice of the early church.

celebrant: The presiding cleric, whether bishop or priest, at the Eucharist, and, by extension, at other sacramental rites, such as baptism.

ceremonial: The actions that take place during worship. Worship is constituted of both rite and ceremonial, word and action.

censer: Vessel in which incense is burned; also called a thurible.

cerecloth: Fabric impregnated with wax and used under the altar linen, originally to protect it from exposure to the oils used to consecrate the altar.

chalice: Cup used for the wine in the Holy Eucharist.

chalicist: The person, ordained or lay, who administers the chalice at Communion.

chancel: Elevated area where the altar and, in some churches, the pulpit/ambo are located.

chapel: 1) A separate church building often founded by a larger congregation as a mission and usually supported by it; 2) An area of a church with its own seating and altar, often used for smaller ceremonies and offices.

chaplain: 1) A minister who serves in an institution such as a hospital, prison, or school with particular care for the patients, prisoners, or students; 2) A deacon or priest (or sometimes lay person) who accompanies and assists a bishop during a liturgy.

chasuble: (CHAH-zuh-bel) The principal vestment for the Eucharistic liturgy; worn like a poncho by the priest or bishop over alb and stole.

chimere: A vestment resembling a long sleeveless vest, usually open at the front, worn by a bishop over the rochet. Usually red or black.

choir: 1) The group of singers who minister in the liturgy; 2) The area of the church in which the singers and other ministers are seated, usually between the nave and the sanctuary, but in some churches in the apse.

chorister: Member of a choir.

chrism: (krizm) Fragrant oil blessed by a bishop and used for anointing in Holy Baptism.

Christ the King: A common name for the last Sunday of the church year, the last Sunday after Pentecost, the proper for which celebrates the sovereignty of Christ.

Christmas: Principal feast of the church year which celebrates Christ's birth; also known as the Nativity of Our Lord.

ciborium: (sih-BOR-ee-um) Covered vessel that holds bread for the Holy Communion.

cincture: (SINK-chur) Rope belt worn with an alb, or a band of fabric worn with a cassock.

coadjutor bishop: A bishop who is elected to succeed as diocesan, but who begins ministry before the resignation or retirement of the preceding diocesan.

collect: (CAW-lect) (n) A prayer that addresses God, describes an attribute of God or a situation, and bids a petition, ending with an invocation of mediation; often used after a set of intercessions to "collect" and conclude them, and at the opening of a liturgy.

columbarium: (CAW-lum-BAAH-ree-yum) Wall or other structure with niches in which ashes from cremation are placed. From the Latin for "dove-cote."

common: (n) A set of liturgical texts (collect, preface, readings) that can be used for various observances, for which a set of unique texts (a *proper*) have not been provided.

Compline: (KAHM-plin) From the Latin for "completion," referring to the prayers that complete the day's worship. An order for night prayer used as the last office before bed.

confirmation: A pastoral rite, consisting of a reaffirmation of baptismal vows, with a blessing and the laying on of hands by a bishop.

consecration: The setting apart of something or someone for holy purposes; said of the bread and wine in Communion, ordinands, and church buildings.

cope: Long cape worn by worship leader, lay or ordained, for certain processions and ceremonial occasions.

corporal: Square white linen cloth placed on the center of the altar, on which the Eucharistic vessels are placed for the celebration of Holy Communion.

corpus: Latin for "body." Carved figure of Christ attached to a cross; together, cross and corpus are a crucifix.

cotta: (KOTT-ah) Short white vestment worn over a cassock by acolytes and choir members.

credence: (KREE-dentz) Shelf or table near the altar which holds sacramental vessels ready for use.

crosier: (KROH-zher) Staff often carried by a bishop in his/her own diocese as a sign of shepherding authority.

crucifer: The acolyte who carries the processional cross.

crucifix: Cross with a corpus attached.

cruciform: (adj) Constructed in the shape of a cross; typical of many church buildings of the gothic type.

cruet: Glass vessel containing wine or water for the Holy Communion. Sometimes used for oil when anointing.

curate: A title usually used for assistant clergy in a parish who serve under the direction of the rector.

Daily Office: The daily liturgies of readings and prayer, including Morning Prayer, Noonday Prayer, Evening Prayer, and Compline.

dalmatic: A vestment, rectangular in shape, with loose short sleeves, worn by a deacon at the Eucharist.

deacon: Member of an order of the ordained ministry, charged particularly with a servant role on behalf of those in need, and to assist bishops and priests in the proclamation of the Gospel and the administration of the sacraments. A "transitional deacon" is one in the process of preparation for ordination as a priest.

dean: 1) Leader of a deanery; 2) Chief cleric of a cathedral.

deanery: A subdivision of a diocese usually consisting of several parishes, sometimes led by a dean.

Deuterocanonical: Another name for the Biblical Apocrypha.

diocesan bishop: The sole or principal bishop of a diocese.

dossal: Fabric mounted on the wall or on posts behind an altar.

east, liturgical: The direction to the rear of the altar, regardless of geographical east.

Easter: Principal season of the church year which celebrates Christ's resurrection. Easter Day (which occurs between March 22 and April 25) is known as the Sunday of the Resurrection and as the "queen of feasts." The Easter season lasts for 50 days, a "week of weeks" plus the Day of Pentecost.

Easter Vigil: Festive liturgy on Easter Eve that includes the lighting of the new fire and procession of the paschal candle, readings from Scripture, Holy Baptism with the renewal of baptismal vows, and the first Eucharist of Easter.

eastward facing altar: An altar set along the liturgical east.

eastward position: A celebration of the Holy Eucharist in which the celebrant and congregation face liturgical east together during portions of the Eucharistic Prayer addressed to God.

Ecclesiasticus: One of the Deuterocanonical books (or Apocrypha); called "Sirach" in some translations.

elements: The physical things used in the celebration of the sacraments: bread and wine in Holy Communion, and water in Holy Baptism.

Epiphany: Principal feast celebrated on January 6, marking the visit of the Magi to Jesus and the consequent revelation of Christ to the world.

Eucharist: (YOO-kar-ist) From the Greek for "thanksgiving"; a name for the Holy Communion. The sacrament of Word, bread, and wine (in which the elements convey the Body and Blood of our Lord) for which we give thanks, and through which we are nourished and strengthened in Christ's name and sustained in baptismal unity in him.

Evening Prayer: An evening worship liturgy of Scripture readings and prayer; also known as Vespers.

ewer: (YOO-er) A pitcher of water used at the baptismal font.

fair linen: Top white linen cloth covering the altar and thus serving as the table cloth for the Holy Eucharist.

flagon: (FLAG-un) Pitcher-like vessel from which wine is poured into the chalice for the Holy Eucharist.

font: From the Latin for "fountain"; the pool or basin that holds water for Holy Baptism.

fraction: Ceremonial breaking of the bread in the Holy Communion liturgy.

free-standing altar: An altar behind which the priest or bishop stands (facing the congregation) during the celebration of the Eucharist.

friar: A man who has made religious vows in a community; from the Latin for "brother." The first friars were Franciscan and Dominican.

frontal: Fabric hanging that covers the entire front of the altar, usually in a seasonal liturgical color; *see also* Laudian frontal.

funeral pall: Large cloth cover draped on a casket when brought into the church for the burial liturgy. If an urn is used for ashes, a small pall is often used to cover it.

Gloria: An ancient hymn of praise sung at the beginning of the Holy Eucharist in Christmastide and at other festive times, and as a canticle in the Daily Office; it begins with the angels' song to the shepherds, "Glory to God. . . ."

Gloria Patri: The closing attribution of all glory to God in the Trinity of Persons, used at the end of Psalms and some canticles in the Daily Office.

gold: Liturgical color for Easter Day as an option to white, giving special prominence to this single most important feast of the year.

Good Friday: The Friday in Holy Week that observes Christ's crucifixion and death.

Gospel side: The left side of the sanctuary, when facing the altar. So called due to the tradition of reading the Gospel from that position.

gradine: The step or shelf at the rear of an eastward facing altar.

Greek cross: Ancient form of the cross in which the four arms are of equal length.

green: Liturgical color for the seasons after Epiphany and Pentecost; symbolic of growth in the Christian way of life.

Holy Trinity: The doctrine of One God in three persons: Father, Son, and Holy Spirit.

Holy Water: Water that has been blessed for use in baptism or for use in the blessing of persons, places, or things. Some churches are equipped with a *stoup* in which water is available for persons to dip a finger and make the sign of the cross as a reminder of their baptism.

Holy Week: The week beginning on the Sunday of the Passion/Palm Sunday and ending with Holy Saturday, recalling the events of the last days of Christ's life.

host: Wafer, made of unleavened bread, for the Holy Eucharist.

icon: An image of Christ or a saint of the church, thought of as more than a mere picture, but as a "window into heaven." Often handwritten with egg-tempera and pigments, with gold-leaf adornment.

incense: Mixture of resins for ceremonial burning, symbolic of our prayers rising to God (see Psalm 141); one of the gifts of the Magi to Jesus on the Epiphany.

intinction: From the Latin for "to dip"; the practice of receiving the Eucharistic elements by dipping the host into the wine.

Kyrie: An invocation of mercy sung or said during the Eucharist and the Offices of Noonday and Compline; it can be in Greek or English, and in threefold, sixfold, or ninefold forms.

Laudian frontal: A type of frontal that entirely covers all sides of an altar (to the floor).

lavabo: (lah-VAH-boh) The point in the Eucharist when the celebrant, and other ministers, wash their hands; from the Latin, "I will wash."

lavabo bowl/towel: Bowl and cloth used for the act of cleansing the celebrant and other ministers' hands in the Eucharist or after the imposition of ashes or oil.

lectern: Reading stand from which the Scripture readings may be proclaimed.

lectionary: The appointed system of Scripture readings for the days of the church year. Also refers to the book that contains these readings.

lector: One who reads the first and second readings from Scripture in the Eucharistic liturgy, or the biblical readings in other rites.

Lent: From the Anglo-Saxon for "spring"; the penitential 40-day season (excluding Sundays) before Easter, beginning with Ash Wednesday. Symbolic of Christ's 40 days in the wilderness. Lent is traditionally the season when candidates prepare for Holy Baptism at the Easter Vigil.

Lenten veil: Cloth used to cover crosses, sculpture, pictures, and other objects during Lent.

linens: Refers to all of the various white fabrics used in the sanctuary and in other rites: altar linens, communion linens (corporal, pall, and purificator), and other linens (covers for the credence and offertory tables, lavabo towel, and baptismal towel).

litany: A form of prayer sung responsively between a leader and the congregation; the Great Litany is one of the first liturgical compositions in English and is used in its present form during Lent or in times of crisis; there is also a Litany for Ordinations addressing the particular concerns of the church with prayer for those being ordained.

liturgy: From the Greek for "public works" (that is, work undertaken on behalf of the whole people); the worship of the church in general, or any particular worship service.

Liturgy of the Word: That portion of the Eucharistic liturgy preceding the communion, focused on the reading, hearing, and exposition of Scripture.

Magnificat: (mahg-NIFF-ih-kaht) Latin title for the Song of Mary, "My soul proclaims the greatness of the Lord," which is a canticle at Evening Prayer, and is from Luke 1:46–55.

matins: (MAT-ins) From the Latin for "morning"; morning liturgy of Scripture reading and prayer; also known as Morning Prayer. Sometimes spelled *mattins*.

Maundy Thursday: (MAWN-dee) From the Latin *mandatum* for "commandment"; the Thursday in Holy Week which commemorates the institution of the Holy Communion at the Last Supper, during which Jesus commanded his disciples to love one another and washed their feet. The footwashing itself is sometimes called "the Maundy."

memorial garden: Usually a courtyard garden on church property in which ashes are interred or scattered after cremation.

mensa: The top surface of an altar (from the Latin for "table").

mixed chalice: So called from the custom of adding a small amount of water to the wine administered at the Eucharist.

miter: (MY-ter) From the Greek for "headband"; a liturgical hat worn by a bishop.

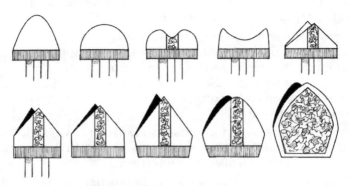

Miters go on top of bishops. They've been wearing them a long time.

monk: A man who has made monastic vows in a religious community, usually devoted to prayer and manual work in the monastery.

Morning Prayer: Morning liturgy of Scripture reading and prayer; also known as matins.

narthex: Entrance hall, lobby, or gathering space of a church building which leads to the nave.

nave: From the Latin for "ship"; the section of the church building between the narthex and the chancel, where the congregation assembles for worship.

new fire: The fire kindled on Easter Eve, used to light the paschal candle for the Easter Vigil. Symbolic of Christ's risen presence.

north, liturgical: The direction to the left when facing the altar. Also called "the Gospel side," due to the traditional reading of the Gospel from that side of the sanctuary.

nun: A woman who has made monastic vows, usually in a contemplative community.

Nunc dimittis: (NOONK dih-MIH-tiss) Latin title for the Song of Simeon, the canticle from Luke 2:29–32, "Lord, you now have set your servant free," used in Evening Prayer and Compline.

oblations: Offerings of bread, wine, and money brought to the altar during the offertory.

offertory: Portion of a liturgical rite when the offerings of the people are received and presented.

office: Any liturgical celebration, but usually used to mean the Daily Office (Morning and Evening Prayer, Noonday Prayer, and Compline).

Ordinal: The ritual appointed for ordination of bishops, priests, and deacons.

ordinary: 1) Those parts of the Eucharistic liturgy that do not change from week to week; 2) The diocesan bishop, usually in the phrase "canon to the ordinary," often a senior priest chosen to work as the bishop's pastoral and/or administrative assistant.

orphrey: (OR-free) Ornamental band or border on a chasuble or other vestment or altar hanging.

pall: Linen-covered square placed over rim of the chalice; *see also* funeral pall.

Palm Sunday: *See* Sunday of the Passion.

paraments: Cloth hangings of various seasonal liturgical colors used to adorn the altar and pulpit/ambo/lectern.

Paschal candle: Large candle carried in procession during the Easter Vigil, lit during the Easter season, symbolizing Christ's resurrected presence. At other times of the year, it is placed near the font and lighted for Holy Baptism; may also be placed near the casket during the burial liturgy.

passion red: The deep red liturgical color used in Holy Week. Symbolic of the blood of the passion of Christ.

Paschal candle

paten: (PATT-en) Plate used to hold bread or hosts during the Eucharist.

pectoral cross: A cross on a chain or cord, worn around the neck; normally worn by bishops, and often by members of religious communities.

Pentecost: From the Greek for "fifty"; a principal feast of the church year, occurring 50 days after Easter. Celebrates the descent of the Holy Spirit on the disciples gathered in Jerusalem.

Phos hilaron: (FOHS HILL-uh-ron) Greek for "joyful light"; hence, the Greek name for the canticle in Evening Prayer which begins "O gracious light."

piscina: A special drain in the sacristy which goes directly into the ground, used for disposal of water used to rinse vessels and wash linens after the Holy Communion.

preface: A short text that introduces the Sanctus in the Holy Communion; it varies with and is proper to the season or the celebration.

presider: The bishop or priest who leads the celebration of the Eucharist or another rite.

Presiding Bishop: The primate and chief pastor of the Episcopal Church. Some other churches, including other members of the Anglican Communion, also use this title for their primate or senior bishop.

prie-dieu: (pree-DYOO) French term for the individual or dual (for weddings) kneeler-with-bookrest used in worship services, as well as at other times when kneeling for prayer is desired.

priest: An order of the ordained ministry of the church. Also called a "presbyter."

primate: The principal bishop who is responsible for leadership in a national church; in the Episcopal Church this is the Presiding Bishop, who is elected for a term of nine years.

processional cross: A cross or crucifix on a tall staff used to lead processions.

processional torch: *See* torch.

proper: The varying portion of the Eucharistic liturgy that is appointed for the day (or season) of the church year; that is, the texts "proper" to that day which include the collect of the day, Scripture readings, and preface.

pulpit: Raised reading desk in the chancel from which the Gospel may be read and the sermon preached; *see also* ambo.

purificator: Square, folded linen napkin used to cleanse the edge of the chalice during the distribution of Holy Communion.

purple: Liturgical color for Advent and Lent.

pyx: A small container used to carry Eucharistic Bread to those unable to attend worship due to illness.

rector: A priest who has charge of a parish, usually called by the congregation and instituted by the bishop, and having tenure; responsible for the spiritual oversight of the congregation.

red: Liturgical color, symbolic of the fire of the Holy Spirit. Used on the Day of Pentecost, and feasts of apostles and martyrs.

religious: (n) A general term for one who has taken vows in a community of monks, nuns, brothers, or sisters.

reredos: (RAIR-eh-doss) Carved stone or wood panel behind and above an altar.

reserved sacrament: The portion of Bread (and sometimes Wine) not consumed as part of the Holy Eucharist, but retained in a special repository, often called a tabernacle, for distribution to the sick, and in some traditions, as a focus for devotional practices.

rite: The text of a liturgy. Worship is constituted of both rite and ceremony, word and action.

rochet: Long white vestment (usually with full sleeves gathered at the wrist) worn by bishops under the chimere.

rubric: From the Latin for "red"; a direction for the conduct of a liturgy. Rubrics were usually printed in red. In many modern editions and bulletins, italics are used.

sacraments: Outward and visible signs of inward and spiritual grace, given by Christ, as sure and certain means by which we receive that grace, and as a pledge to assure us of that reception.

sacristy: A room used for storage and preparation of items used in worship; also used for clergy and server vesting before worship.

sanctuary lamp: A candle sometimes suspended from the ceiling or mounted on the chancel wall; in Roman Catholic and some Episcopal churches, it symbolizes the presence of the reserved sacrament.

Sanctus: The song glorifying God beginning "Holy, Holy, Holy" and following the Preface in the Holy Eucharist.

sedilia: In some churches, a set of seats in the sanctuary for the celebrant and assistants.

sign of the cross: Gesture of tracing the outline of the cross with the hand, as a mark of belonging to Christ in Holy Baptism (during which it is first placed on one's forehead).

station: 1) Place from which Communion is administered; 2) One of the fourteen portions of the Way of the Cross.

stole: Cloth band in liturgical color worn over the alb or surplice over a deacon's shoulder, or around a priest's or bishop's neck; signifies the order and office of ministry and the yoke of obedience to Christ.

stoup: Receptacle near the entrance of a church in which holy water is retained for persons to use in making the sign of the cross as a reminder of their baptism.

stripping of the altar: Ceremony at the conclusion of the Maundy Thursday liturgy, in which all appointments, linens, and paraments are removed from the altar and chancel in preparation for Good Friday.

subdeacon: Formerly a member of an order of ministry served prior to ordination as a deacon, now a liturgical office often served by a lay person.

suffragan bishop: A bishop elected to serve in a diocese along with the diocesan, but with tenure.

Sunday of the Passion: The first day of Holy Week, also known as Palm Sunday. Commemorates both Christ's triumphant entry into Jerusalem and his crucifixion.

superfrontal: A short fabric hanging for the front of an altar, used alone or as an additional adornment to a frontal.

surplice: White vestment worn over the cassock; used especially for the Daily Office. The name derives from the Latin for "over the fur" and goes back to the days of unheated churches.

Te Deum laudamus: (tay DAY-um lau-DAH-moos) Latin for "We praise you, God"; a title for the canticle used in Morning Prayer.

Tenebrae: (TENN-eh-bray) From the Latin for "shadows"; a liturgy of Holy Week, in which candles on a special stand are extinguished one by one.

thurible: Vessel in which incense is burned; also known as a censer.

thurible

thurifer: The person who carries the thurible.

torch: Large candle on a staff carried in processions, often flanking the processional cross or gospel book.

torchbearer: An acolyte who carries a processional torch.

Transfiguration: Feast celebrated on August 6, recalling Christ's transfiguration on the mountain.

Triduum: (TRIH-doo-um) Latin for "three days"; the three sacred days from Maundy Thursday evening through Easter Eve, which together celebrate the unity of the Paschal mystery of Christ's death and resurrection.

Trinity Sunday: The First Sunday after Pentecost on which the church celebrates God as the Holy Trinity.

torch

Trisagion: A prayer invoking the mercy of the Holy, Mighty, and Eternal God, sung or said as part of the Eucharist or at other times.

tunicle: A vestment similar to a dalmatic, worn by a subdeacon.

unction: The action of anointing a person with oil.

veil: Cloth placed over sacramental vessels before and after the celebration of Holy Communion.

versicle and response: Brief lines of Scripture (often from the psalms) sung or said responsively in certain rites, including the Daily Office.

vespers: From the Latin for "evening"; an evening liturgy of Scripture readings and prayer. Also known as Evening Prayer.

vestry: The lay governing body of a parish, responsible for the maintenance of the buildings and property, and for finances. (Formerly another name for the sacristy, or place in which clergy vested.)

vicar: A priest who serves at the direction and appointment of the bishop in a mission congregation. Occasionally a curate serving in a mission founded by a larger parish, under the direction of its rector; from the Latin for "in the place of."

vigil: A liturgy held on the eve of a feast, such as the Easter Vigil.

warden: A senior lay leader of a congregation, having specific legal and ecclesiastical responsibilities.

Way of the Cross: A ritual commemorating the Passion of Christ, consisting of fourteen stations, often marked with an image of each event, consisting of a Scriptural passage, versicle and response, and prayer; often used as a Lenten devotion, it appears in the Book of Occasional Services.

white: Liturgical color for Easter Day and Christmas, giving special prominence to these most important feasts. Gold may also be used.

zucchetto: A skull-cap or small circular cap that fits the top of the head, worn by some clergy and members of religious communities; some bishops wear a purple zucchetto.

PRAYER BOOK STUFF

with some brief comments

THE BAPTISMAL COVENANT

The Baptismal Covenant represents a verbal commitment to Christ, in the form of a dialogue between the celebrant and the people. The first part recovers the dialogue form of the Apostles' Creed, and the concluding five questions represent the pledge of commitment to the essentials of a vibrant faith and life in Christ: the teaching and fellowship of the church, prayer, repentance, witness, service, and justice. The Baptismal Covenant is used as a part of the Baptismal liturgy (BCP 304), which is especially appropriate at the Easter Vigil, the Day of Pentecost, All Saints' Day or the following Sunday, and on the Feast of the Baptism of Our Lord. When there are no candidates for Baptism on those days, the Baptismal Covenant may be recited as a renewal of the promises made in Baptism, taking the place of the Nicene Creed (BCP 292).

Celebrant Do you believe in God the Father?

People I believe in God, the Father almighty,
      creator of heaven and earth.

Celebrant Do you believe in Jesus Christ, the Son of God?

People I believe in Jesus Christ, his only Son, our Lord.
      He was conceived by the power of the
          Holy Spirit and born of the Virgin Mary.
      He suffered under Pontius Pilate,
          was crucified, died, and was buried.
      He descended to the dead.
      On the third day he rose again.
      He ascended into heaven,
          and is seated at the right hand of the Father.
      He will come again to judge the living and
          the dead.

Celebrant   Do you believe in God the Holy Spirit?

People   I believe in the Holy Spirit,
      the holy catholic Church,
      the communion of saints,
      the forgiveness of sins,
      the resurrection of the body,
      and the life everlasting.

Celebrant   Will you continue in the apostles' teaching and fellow-ship, in the breaking of bread, and in the prayers?

People   I will, with God's help.

Celebrant   Will you persevere in resisting evil, and, whenever you fall into sin, repent and return to the Lord?

People   I will, with God's help.

Celebrant   Will you proclaim by word and example the Good News of God in Christ?

People   I will, with God's help.

Celebrant   Will you seek and serve Christ in all persons, loving your neighbor as yourself?

People   I will, with God's help.

Celebrant   Will you strive for justice and peace among all people, and respect the dignity of every human being?

People   I will, with God's help.

AN OUTLINE OF THE FAITH COMMONLY CALLED THE CATECHISM

(Book of Common Prayer, pages 845–862)

The Catechism is intended to be used as a summary of the Christian faith as Episcopalians understand it. It takes the form of a commentary on the creeds—themselves even more concise summaries of the basics of Christianity. Unlike the catechisms or books of doctrine used in some other Christian traditions, it is relatively short and to the point, and is best used as a discussion starter or teaching tool; though it also serves as a quick outline for an inquiring stranger. As William Reed Huntington (see page 78) once wrote, "My whole effort in connection with the doctrinal legislation of the Episcopal Church has been to reduce the required dogma to a minimum, while yet insisting upon that minimum. What has ailed the Church, it seems to me, has been, not the *principle* of dogma, but the multiplication of *dogmas*." The Catechism can be seen as an example of this heritage.

Human Nature

Q. What are we by nature?

A. We are part of God's creation, made in the image of God.

Q. What does it mean to be created in the image of God?

A. It means that we are free to make choices: to love, to create, to reason, and to live in harmony with creation and with God.

Q. Why then do we live apart from God and out of harmony with creation?

A. From the beginning, human beings have misused their freedom and made wrong choices.

Q. Why do we not use our freedom as we should?

A. Because we rebel against God, and we put ourselves in the place of God.

Q. What help is there for us?

A. Our help is in God.

Q. How did God first help us?

A. God first helped us by revealing himself and his will, through nature and history, through many seers and saints, and especially through the prophets of Israel.

God the Father

Q. What do we learn about God as creator from the revelation to Israel?

A. We learn that there is one God, the Father Almighty, creator of heaven and earth, of all that is, seen and unseen.

Q. What does this mean?

A. This means that the universe is good, that it is the work of a single loving God who creates, sustains, and directs it.

Q. What does this mean about our place in the universe?

A. It means that the world belongs to its creator; and that we are called to enjoy it and to care for it in accordance with God's purposes.

Q. What does this mean about human life?

A. It means that all people are worthy of respect and honor, because all are created in the image of God, and all can respond to the love of God.

Q. How was this revelation handed down to us?

A. This revelation was handed down to us through a community created by a covenant with God.

The Old Covenant

Q. What is meant by a covenant with God?

A. A covenant is a relationship initiated by God, to which
a body of people responds in faith.

Q. What is the Old Covenant?

A. The Old Covenant is the one given by God to the Hebrew
people.

Q. What did God promise them?

A. God promised that they would be his people to bring all the
nations of the world to him.

Q. What response did God require from the chosen people?

A. God required the chosen people to be faithful; to love justice,
to do mercy, and to walk humbly with their God.

Q. Where is this Old Covenant to be found?

A. The covenant with the Hebrew people is to be found in the
books which we call the Old Testament.

Q. Where in the Old Testament is God's will for us shown
most clearly?

A. God's will for us is shown most clearly in the Ten
Commandments.

The Ten Commandments

Q. What are the Ten Commandments?

A. The Ten Commandments are the laws given to Moses and the
people of Israel.

Q. What do we learn from these commandments?

A. We learn two things: our duty to God, and our duty to our
neighbors.

Q. What is our duty to God?

A. Our duty is to believe and trust in God;

    I To love and obey God and to bring others to know him;

   II To put nothing in the place of God;

  III To show God respect in thought, word, and deed;

  IV And to set aside regular times for worship, prayer, and the study of God's ways.

Q. What is our duty to our neighbors?

A. Our duty to our neighbors is to love them as ourselves, and to do to other people as we wish them to do to us;

   V To love, honor, and help our parents and family; to honor those in authority, and to meet their just demands;

  VI To show respect for the life God has given us; to work and pray for peace; to bear no malice, prejudice, or hatred in our hearts; and to be kind to all the creatures of God;

  VII To use all our bodily desires as God intended;

VIII To be honest and fair in our dealings; to seek justice, freedom, and the necessities of life for all people; and to use our talents and possessions as ones who must answer for them to God;

  IX To speak the truth, and not to mislead others by our silence;

   X To resist temptations to envy, greed, and jealousy; to rejoice in other people's gifts and graces; and to do our duty for the love of God, who has called us into fellowship with him.

Q. What is the purpose of the Ten Commandments?

A. The Ten Commandments were given to define our relationship with God and our neighbors.

Q. Since we do not fully obey them, are they useful at all?

A. Since we do not fully obey them, we see more clearly our sin and our need for redemption.

Sin and Redemption

Q. What is sin?

A. Sin is the seeking of our own will instead of the will of God, thus distorting our relationship with God, with other people, and with all creation.

Q. How does sin have power over us?

A. Sin has power over us because we lose our liberty when our relationship with God is distorted.

Q. What is redemption?

A. Redemption is the act of God which sets us free from the power of evil, sin, and death.

Q. How did God prepare us for redemption?

A. God sent the prophets to call us back to himself, to show us our need for redemption, and to announce the coming of the Messiah.

Q. What is meant by the Messiah?

A. The Messiah is one sent by God to free us from the power of sin, so that with the help of God we may live in harmony with God, within ourselves, with our neighbors, and with all creation.

Q. Who do we believe is the Messiah?

A. The Messiah, or Christ, is Jesus of Nazareth, the only Son of God.

God the Son

Q. What do we mean when we say that Jesus is the only Son of God?

A. We mean that Jesus is the only perfect image of the Father, and shows us the nature of God.

Q. What is the nature of God revealed in Jesus?

A. God is love.

Q. What do we mean when we say that Jesus was conceived by the power of the Holy Spirit and became incarnate from the Virgin Mary?

A. We mean that by God's own act, his divine Son received our human nature from the Virgin Mary, his mother.

Q. Why did he take our human nature?

A. The divine Son became human, so that in him human beings might be adopted as children of God, and be made heirs of God's kingdom.

Q. What is the great importance of Jesus' suffering and death?

A. By his obedience, even to suffering and death, Jesus made the offering which we could not make; in him we are freed from the power of sin and reconciled to God.

Q. What is the significance of Jesus' resurrection?

A. By his resurrection, Jesus overcame death and opened for us the way of eternal life.

Q. What do we mean when we say that he descended to the dead?

A. We mean that he went to the departed and offered them also the benefits of redemption.

Q. What do we mean when we say that he ascended into heaven and is seated at the right hand of the Father?

A. We mean that Jesus took our human nature into heaven where he now reigns with the Father and intercedes for us.

Q. How can we share in his victory over sin, suffering, and death?

A. We share in his victory when we are baptized into the New Covenant and become living members of Christ.

The New Covenant

Q. What is the New Covenant?

A. The New Covenant is the new relationship with God given by Jesus Christ, the Messiah, to the apostles; and, through them, to all who believe in him.

Q. What did the Messiah promise in the New Covenant?

A. Christ promised to bring us into the kingdom of God and give us life in all its fullness.

Q. What response did Christ require?

A. Christ commanded us to believe in him and to keep his commandments.

Q. What are the commandments taught by Christ?

A. Christ taught us the Summary of the Law and gave us the New Commandment.

Q. What is the Summary of the Law?

A. You shall love the Lord your God with all your heart, with all your soul, and with all your mind. This is the first and the great commandment. And the second is like it: You shall love your neighbor as yourself.

Q. What is the New Commandment?

A. The New Commandment is that we love one another as Christ loved us.

Q. Where may we find what Christians believe about Christ?

A. What Christians believe about Christ is found in the Scriptures and summed up in the creeds.

The Creeds

Q. What are the creeds?

A. The creeds are statements of our basic beliefs about God.

Q. How many creeds does this Church use in its worship?

A. This Church uses two creeds: The Apostles' Creed and the Nicene Creed.

Q. What is the Apostles' Creed?

A. The Apostles' Creed is the ancient creed of Baptism; it is used in the Church's daily worship to recall our Baptismal Covenant.

Q. What is the Nicene Creed?

A. The Nicene Creed is the creed of the universal Church and is used at the Eucharist.

Q. What, then, is the Athanasian Creed?

A. The Athanasian Creed is an ancient document proclaiming the nature of the Incarnation and of God as Trinity.

Q. What is the Trinity?

A. The Trinity is one God: Father, Son, and Holy Spirit.

The Holy Spirit

Q. Who is the Holy Spirit?

A. The Holy Spirit is the Third Person of the Trinity, God at work in the world and in the Church even now.

Q. How is the Holy Spirit revealed in the Old Covenant?

A. The Holy Spirit is revealed in the Old Covenant as the giver of life, the One who spoke through the prophets.

Q. How is the Holy Spirit revealed in the New Covenant?

A. The Holy Spirit is revealed as the Lord who leads us into all truth and enables us to grow in the likeness of Christ.

Q. How do we recognize the presence of the Holy Spirit in our lives?

A. We recognize the presence of the Holy Spirit when we confess Jesus Christ as Lord and are brought into love and harmony with God, with ourselves, with our neighbors, and with all creation.

Q. How do we recognize the truths taught by the Holy Spirit?

A. We recognize truths to be taught by the Holy Spirit when they are in accord with the Scriptures.

The Holy Scriptures

Q. What are the Holy Scriptures?

A. The Holy Scriptures, commonly called the Bible, are the books of the Old and New Testaments; other books, called the Apocrypha, are often included in the Bible.

Q. What is the Old Testament?

A. The Old Testament consists of books written by the people of the Old Covenant, under the inspiration of the Holy Spirit, to show God at work in nature and history.

Q. What is the New Testament?

A. The New Testament consists of books written by the people of the New Covenant, under the inspiration of the Holy Spirit, to set forth the life and teachings of Jesus and to proclaim the Good News of the Kingdom for all people.

Q. What is the Apocrypha?

A. The Apocrypha is a collection of additional books written by people of the Old Covenant, and used in the Christian Church.

Q. Why do we call the Holy Scriptures the Word of God?

A. We call them the Word of God because God inspired their human authors and because God still speaks to us through the Bible.

Q. How do we understand the meaning of the Bible?

A. We understand the meaning of the Bible by the help of the Holy Spirit, who guides the Church in the true interpretation of the Scriptures.

The Church

Q. What is the Church?

A. The Church is the community of the New Covenant.

Q. How is the Church described in the Bible?

A. The Church is described as the Body of which Jesus Christ is the Head and of which all baptized persons are members. It is called the People of God, the New Israel, a holy nation, a royal priesthood, and the pillar and ground of truth.

Q. How is the Church described in the creeds?

A. The Church is described as one, holy, catholic, and apostolic.

Q. Why is the Church described as one?

A. The Church is one, because it is one Body, under one Head, our Lord Jesus Christ.

Q. Why is the Church described as holy?

A. The Church is holy, because the Holy Spirit dwells in it, consecrates its members, and guides them to do God's work.

Q. Why is the Church described as catholic?

A. The Church is catholic, because it proclaims the whole Faith to all people, to the end of time.

Q. Why is the Church described as apostolic?

A. The Church is apostolic, because it continues in the teaching and fellowship of the apostles and is sent to carry out Christ's mission to all people.

Q. What is the mission of the Church?

A. The mission of the Church is to restore all people to unity with God and each other in Christ.

Q. How does the Church pursue its mission?

A. The Church pursues its mission as it prays and worships, proclaims the Gospel, and promotes justice, peace, and love.

Q. Through whom does the Church carry out its mission?

A. The Church carries out its mission through the ministry of all its members.

The Ministry

Q. Who are the ministers of the Church?

A. The ministers of the Church are lay persons, bishops, priests, and deacons.

Q. What is the ministry of the laity?

A. The ministry of lay persons is to represent Christ and his Church; to bear witness to him wherever they may be and, according to the gifts given them, to carry on Christ's work of reconciliation in the world; and to take their place in the life, worship, and governance of the Church.

Q. What is the ministry of a bishop?

A. The ministry of a bishop is to represent Christ and his Church, particularly as apostle, chief priest, and pastor of a diocese; to guard the faith, unity, and discipline of the whole Church; to proclaim the Word of God; to act in Christ's name for the reconciliation of the world and the building up of the Church; and to ordain others to continue Christ's ministry.

Q. What is the ministry of a priest or presbyter?

A. The ministry of a priest is to represent Christ and his Church, particularly as pastor to the people; to share with the bishop in the overseeing of the Church; to proclaim the Gospel; to administer the sacraments; and to bless and declare pardon in the name of God.

Q. What is the ministry of a deacon?

A. The ministry of a deacon is to represent Christ and his Church, particularly as a servant of those in need; and to assist bishops and priests in the proclamation of the Gospel and the administration of the sacraments.

Q. What is the duty of all Christians?

A. The duty of all Christians is to follow Christ; to come together week by week for corporate worship; and to work, pray, and give for the spread of the kingdom of God.

Prayer and Worship

Q. What is prayer?

A. Prayer is responding to God, by thought and by deeds, with or without words.

Q. What is Christian Prayer?

A. Christian prayer is response to God the Father, through Jesus Christ, in the power of the Holy Spirit.

Q. What prayer did Christ teach us?

A. Our Lord gave us the example of prayer known as the Lord's Prayer.

Q. What are the principal kinds of prayer?

A. The principal kinds of prayer are adoration, praise, thanksgiving, penitence, oblation, intercession, and petition.

Q. What is adoration?

A. Adoration is the lifting up of the heart and mind to God, asking nothing but to enjoy God's presence.

Q. Why do we praise God?

A. We praise God, not to obtain anything, but because God's Being draws praise from us.

Q. For what do we offer thanksgiving?

A. Thanksgiving is offered to God for all the blessings of this life, for our redemption, and for whatever draws us closer to God.

Q. What is penitence?

A. In penitence, we confess our sins and make restitution where possible, with the intention to amend our lives.

Q. What is prayer of oblation?

A. Oblation is an offering of ourselves, our lives and labors, in union with Christ, for the purposes of God.

Q. What are intercession and petition?

A. Intercession brings before God the needs of others; in petition, we present our own needs, that God's will may be done.

Q. What is corporate worship?

A. In corporate worship, we unite ourselves with others to acknowledge the holiness of God, to hear God's Word, to offer prayer, and to celebrate the sacraments.

The Sacraments

Q. What are the sacraments?

A. The sacraments are outward and visible signs of inward and spiritual grace, given by Christ as sure and certain means by which we receive that grace.

Q. What is grace?

A. Grace is God's favor toward us, unearned and undeserved; by grace God forgives our sins, enlightens our minds, stirs our hearts, and strengthens our wills.

Q. What are the two great sacraments of the Gospel?

A. The two great sacraments given by Christ to his Church are Holy Baptism and the Holy Eucharist.

Holy Baptism

Q. What is Holy Baptism?

A. Holy Baptism is the sacrament by which God adopts us as his children and makes us members of Christ's Body, the Church, and inheritors of the kingdom of God.

Q. What is the outward and visible sign in Baptism?

A. The outward and visible sign in Baptism is water, in which the person is baptized in the Name of the Father, and of the Son, and of the Holy Spirit.

Q. What is the inward and spiritual grace in Baptism?

A. The inward and spiritual grace in Baptism is union with Christ in his death and resurrection, birth into God's family the Church, forgiveness of sins, and new life in the Holy Spirit.

Q. What is required of us at Baptism?

A. It is required that we renounce Satan, repent of our sins, and accept Jesus as our Lord and Savior.

Q. Why then are infants baptized?

A. Infants are baptized so that they can share citizenship in the Covenant, membership in Christ, and redemption by God.

Q. How are the promises for infants made and carried out?

A. Promises are made for them by their parents and sponsors, who guarantee that the infants will be brought up within the Church, to know Christ and be able to follow him.

The Holy Eucharist

Q. What is the Holy Eucharist?

A. The Holy Eucharist is the sacrament commanded by Christ for the continual remembrance of his life, death, and resurrection, until his coming again.

Q. Why is the Eucharist called a sacrifice?

A. Because the Eucharist, the Church's sacrifice of praise and thanksgiving, is the way by which the sacrifice of Christ is made present, and in which he unites us to his one offering of himself.

Q. By what other names is this service known?

A. The Holy Eucharist is called the Lord's Supper, and Holy Communion; it is also known as the Divine Liturgy, the Mass, and the Great Offering.

Q. What is the outward and visible sign in the Eucharist?

A. The outward and visible sign in the Eucharist is bread and wine, given and received according to Christ's command.

Q. What is the inward and spiritual grace given in the Eucharist?

A. The inward and spiritual grace in the Holy Communion is the Body and Blood of Christ given to his people, and received by faith.

Q. What are the benefits which we receive in the Lord's Supper?

A. The benefits we receive are the forgiveness of our sins, the strengthening of our union with Christ and one another, and the foretaste of the heavenly banquet which is our nourishment in eternal life.

Q. What is required of us when we come to the Eucharist?

A. It is required that we should examine our lives, repent of our sins, and be in love and charity with all people.

Other Sacramental Rites

Q. What other sacramental rites evolved in the Church under the guidance of the Holy Spirit?

A. Other sacramental rites which evolved in the Church include confirmation, ordination, holy matrimony, reconciliation of a penitent, and unction.

Q. How do they differ from the two sacraments of the Gospel?

A. Although they are means of grace, they are not necessary for all persons in the same way that Baptism and the Eucharist are.

Q. What is Confirmation?

A. Confirmation is the rite in which we express a mature commitment to Christ, and receive strength from the Holy Spirit through prayer and the laying on of hands by a bishop.

Q. What is required of those to be confirmed?

A. It is required of those to be confirmed that they have been baptized, are sufficiently instructed in the Christian Faith, are penitent for their sins, and are ready to affirm their confession of Jesus Christ as Savior and Lord.

Q. What is Ordination?

A. Ordination is the rite in which God gives authority and the grace of the Holy Spirit to those being made bishops, priests, and deacons, through prayer and the laying on of hands by bishops.

Q. What is Holy Matrimony?

A. Holy Matrimony is Christian marriage, in which the woman and man enter into a life-long union, make their vows before God and the Church, and receive the grace and blessing of God to help them fulfill their vows.

Q. What is Reconciliation of a Penitent?

A. Reconciliation of a Penitent, or Penance, is the rite in which those who repent of their sins may confess them to God in the presence of a priest, and receive the assurance of pardon and the grace of absolution.

Q. What is Unction of the Sick?

A. Unction is the rite of anointing the sick with oil, or the laying on of hands, by which God's grace is given for the healing of spirit, mind, and body.

Q. Is God's activity limited to these rites?

A. God does not limit himself to these rites; they are patterns of countless ways by which God uses material things to reach out to us.

Q. How are the sacraments related to our Christian hope?

A. Sacraments sustain our present hope and anticipate its future fulfillment.

The Christian Hope

Q. What is the Christian hope?

A. The Christian hope is to live with confidence in newness and fullness of life, and to await the coming of Christ in glory, and the completion of God's purpose for the world.

Q. What do we mean by the coming of Christ in glory?

A. By the coming of Christ in glory, we mean that Christ will come, not in weakness but in power, and will make all things new.

Q. What do we mean by heaven and hell?

A. By heaven, we mean eternal life in our enjoyment of God; by hell, we mean eternal death in our rejection of God.

Q. Why do we pray for the dead?

A. We pray for them, because we still hold them in our love, and because we trust that in God's presence those who have chosen to serve him will grow in his love, until they see him as he is.

Q. What do we mean by the last judgment?

A. We believe that Christ will come in glory and judge the living and the dead.

Q. What do we mean by the resurrection of the body?

A. We mean that God will raise us from death in the fullness of our being, that we may live with Christ in the communion of the saints.

Q. What is the communion of saints?

A. The communion of saints is the whole family of God, the living and the dead, those whom we love and those whom we hurt, bound together in Christ by sacrament, prayer, and praise.

Q. What do we mean by everlasting life?

A. By everlasting life, we mean a new existence, in which we are united with all the people of God, in the joy of fully knowing and loving God and each other.

Q. What, then, is our assurance as Christians?

A. Our assurance as Christians is that nothing, not even death, shall separate us from the love of God which is in Christ Jesus our Lord. Amen.

THE TEN COMMANDMENTS
(Book of Common Prayer, page 350)

The Ten Commandments, or Decalogue, appears in both traditional and modern language versions. There is also an expanded summary as part of the Catechism (BCP 847). The liturgical forms are commended for use in worship, recited as part of the Penitential Order.

Hear the commandments of God to his people:
I am the Lord your God who brought you out of bondage.
You shall have no other gods but me.
Amen. Lord have mercy.

You shall not make for yourself any idol.
Amen. Lord have mercy.

You shall not invoke with malice the Name of the Lord your God.
Amen. Lord have mercy.

Remember the Sabbath Day and keep it holy.
Amen. Lord have mercy.

Honor your father and your mother.
Amen. Lord have mercy.

You shall not commit murder.
Amen. Lord have mercy.

You shall not commit adultery.
Amen. Lord have mercy.

You shall not steal.
Amen. Lord have mercy.

You shall not be a false witness.
Amen. Lord have mercy.

You shall not covet anything that belongs to your neighbor.
Amen. Lord have mercy.

THE LORD'S PRAYER

(Book of Common Prayer, page 364)

Traditional

Our Father, who art in heaven,
hallowed be thy Name,
thy kingdom come,
thy will be done,
on earth as it is in heaven.
Give us this day our daily
    bread.
And forgive us our trespasses,
as we forgive those
who trespass against us.
And lead us not into
    temptation,
but deliver us from evil.
For thine is the kingdom,
and the power, and the glory,
for ever and ever. Amen.

Contemporary

Our Father in heaven,
hallowed be your Name,
your kingdom come,
your will be done,
on earth as in heaven.
Give us today our daily bread.
Forgive us our sins
as we forgive those
who sin against us.
Save us from the time of trial,
and deliver us from evil.
For the kingdom, the power,
and the glory are yours,
now and for ever. Amen.

DAILY DEVOTIONS FOR INDIVIDUALS AND FAMILIES

(Book of Common Prayer, pages 136–140)

These devotions follow the basic structure of the Daily Office of the Church.

When more than one person is present, the Reading and the Collect should be read by one person, and the other parts said in unison, or in some other convenient manner. (For suggestions about reading the Psalms, see page 582 of the BCP.)

For convenience, appropriate Psalms, Readings, and Collects are provided in each service. When desired, however, the Collect of the Day, or any of the Collects appointed in the Daily Offices, may be used instead.

The Psalms and Readings may be replaced by those appointed in:

a) the Lectionary for Sundays, Holy Days, the Common of Saints, and Various Occasions (BCP 888),

b) the Daily Office Lectionary (BCP 934), or

c) some other manual of devotion which provides daily selections for the Church Year.

In the Morning

From Psalm 51

Open my lips, O Lord, *
and my mouth shall proclaim your praise.
Create in me a clean heart, O God, *
    and renew a right spirit within me.
Cast me not away from your presence *
    and take not your holy Spirit from me.
Give me the joy of your saving help again *
    and sustain me with your bountiful Spirit.
Glory to the Father, and to the Son, and to the Holy Spirit: *
    as it was in the beginning, is now, and will be for ever. Amen.

A Reading

Blessed be the God and Father of our Lord Jesus Christ! By his great mercy we have been born anew to a living hope through the resurrection of Jesus Christ from the dead. *I Peter 1:3*

A period of silence may follow.

A hymn or canticle may be used; the Apostles' Creed may be said.

Prayers may be offered for ourselves and others.

The Lord's Prayer

The Collect

Lord God, almighty and everlasting Father, you have brought us in safety to this new day: Preserve us with your mighty power, that we may not fall into sin, nor be overcome by adversity; and in all we do, direct us to the fulfilling of your purpose; through Jesus Christ our Lord. *Amen.*

At Noon

From Psalm 113

Give praise, you servants of the Lord; *
  praise the Name of the Lord.
Let the Name of the Lord be blessed, *
  from this time forth for evermore.
From the rising of the sun to its going down *
  let the Name of the Lord be praised.
The Lord is high above all nations, *
  and his glory above the heavens.

A Reading

O God, you will keep in perfect peace those whose minds are fixed on you; for in returning and rest we shall be saved; in quietness and trust shall be our strength. *Isaiah 26:3; 30:15*

Prayers may be offered for ourselves and others.

The Lord's Prayer

The Collect

Blessed Savior, at this hour you hung upon the cross, stretching out your loving arms: Grant that all the peoples of the earth may look to you and be saved; for your mercies' sake. *Amen.*

or this

Lord Jesus Christ, you said to your apostles, "Peace I give to you; my own peace I leave with you": Regard not our sins, but the faith of your Church, and give to us the peace and unity of that heavenly City, where with the Father and the Holy Spirit you live and reign, now and for ever. *Amen.*

In the Early Evening

This devotion may be used before or after the evening meal.

The Order of Worship for the Evening (BCP 109) may be used instead.

O gracious Light,
pure brightness of the everliving Father in heaven,
O Jesus Christ, holy and blessed!

Now as we come to the setting of the sun,
and our eyes behold the vesper light,
we sing your praises O God: Father, Son, and Holy Spirit.

You are worthy at all times to be praised by happy voices,
O Son of God, O Giver of life,
and to be glorified through all the worlds.

A Reading

It is not ourselves that we proclaim; we proclaim Christ Jesus as
Lord, and ourselves as your servants, for Jesus' sake. For the same
God who said, "Out of darkness let light shine," has caused his light
to shine within us, to give the light of revelation—the revelation
of the glory of God in the face of Jesus Christ. *2 Corinthians 4:5–6*

Prayers may be offered for ourselves and others.

The Lord's Prayer

The Collect

Lord Jesus, stay with us, for evening is at hand and the day is past;
be our companion in the way, kindle our hearts, and awaken
hope, that we may know you as you are revealed in Scripture and
the breaking of bread. Grant this for the sake of your love. *Amen.*

At the Close of Day

Psalm 134

Behold now, bless the Lord, all you servants of the Lord, *
    you that stand by night in the house of the Lord.
Lift up your hands in the holy place and bless the Lord; *
    the Lord who made heaven and earth
bless you out of Zion.

A Reading

Lord, you are in the midst of us and we are called by your Name:
Do not forsake us, O Lord our God. *Jeremiah 14:9, 22*

The following may be said.

Lord, you now have set your servant free *
    to go in peace as you have promised;
For these eyes of mine have seen the Savior, *
    whom you have prepared for all the world to see:
A Light to enlighten the nations, *
    and the glory of your people Israel.

*Prayers for ourselves and others may follow. It is appropriate that
prayers of thanksgiving for the blessings of the day, and penitence for
our sins, be included.*

The Lord's Prayer

The Collect

Visit this place, O Lord, and drive far from it all snares of the
enemy; let your holy angels dwell with us to preserve us in peace;
and let your blessing be upon us always; through Jesus Christ our
Lord. *Amen.*

The almighty and merciful Lord, Father, Son, and Holy Spirit, bless
us and keep us. *Amen.*

A SHORT SELECTION OF PRAYERS

(from the Book of Common Prayer, pages as indicated)

For the Human Family (815)

O God, you made us in your own image and redeemed us through Jesus your Son: Look with compassion on the whole human family; take away the arrogance and hatred which infect our hearts; break down the walls that separate us; unite us in bonds of love; and work through our struggle and confusion to accomplish your purposes on earth; that, in your good time, all nations and races may serve you in harmony around your heavenly throne; through Jesus Christ our Lord. *Amen.*

For Peace (815)

Eternal God, in whose perfect kingdom no sword is drawn but the sword of righteousness, no strength known but the strength of love: So mightily spread abroad your Spirit, that all peoples may be gathered under the banner of the Prince of Peace, as children of one Father; to whom be dominion and glory, now and for ever. *Amen.*

For the Church (816)

Gracious Father, we pray for thy holy Catholic Church. Fill it with all truth, in all truth with all peace. Where it is corrupt, purify it; where it is in error, direct it; where in any thing it is amiss, reform it. Where it is right, strengthen it; where it is in want, provide for it; where it is divided, reunite it; for the sake of Jesus Christ thy Son our Savior. *Amen.*

For a Church Convention or Meeting (818)

Almighty and everliving God, source of all wisdom and understanding, be present with those who take counsel [in _____] for the renewal and mission of your Church. Teach us in all things to seek first your honor and glory. Guide us to perceive what is right, and grant us both the courage to pursue it and the grace to accomplish it; through Jesus Christ our Lord. *Amen.*

For those about to be Baptized or to renew their Baptismal Covenant (819)

O God, you prepared your disciples for the coming of the Spirit through the teaching of your Son Jesus Christ: Make the hearts and minds of your servants ready to receive the blessing of the Holy Spirit, that they may be filled with the strength of his presence; through Jesus Christ our Lord. *Amen.*

For Sound Government (821)

The responses in italics may be omitted.

O Lord our Governor, bless the leaders of our land, that we may be a people at peace among ourselves and a blessing to other nations of the earth.

Lord, keep this nation under your care.

To the President and members of the Cabinet, to Governors of States, Mayors of Cities, and to all in administrative authority, grant wisdom and grace in the exercise of their duties.

Give grace to your servants, O Lord.

To Senators and Representatives, and those who make our laws in States, Cities, and Towns, give courage, wisdom, and foresight to provide for the needs of all our people, and to fulfill our obligations in the community of nations.

Give grace to your servants, O Lord.

To the Judges and officers of our Courts, give understanding and integrity, that human rights may be safeguarded and justice served.

Give grace to your servants, O Lord.

And finally, teach our people to rely on your strength and to accept their responsibilities to their fellow citizens, that they may elect trustworthy leaders and make wise decisions for the well-being of our society; that we may serve you faithfully in our generation and honor your holy Name.

For yours is the kingdom, O Lord, and you are exalted as head above all. Amen.

For those in the Armed Forces of our Country (823)

Almighty God, we commend to your gracious care and keeping all the men and women of our armed forces at home and abroad. Defend them day by day with your heavenly grace; strengthen them in their trials and temptations; give them courage to face the perils which beset them; and grant them a sense of your abiding presence wherever they may be; through Jesus Christ our Lord. *Amen.*

In Times of Conflict (824)

O God, you have bound us together in a common life. Help us, in the midst of our struggles for justice and truth, to confront one another without hatred or bitterness, and to work together with mutual forbearance and respect; through Jesus Christ our Lord. *Amen.*

For Knowledge of God's Creation (827)

Almighty and everlasting God, you made the universe with all its marvelous order, its atoms, worlds, and galaxies, and the infinite complexity of living creatures: Grant that, as we probe the mysteries of your creation, we may come to know you more truly, and more surely fulfill our role in your eternal purpose; in the name of Jesus Christ our Lord. *Amen.*

For Families (828)

Almighty God, our heavenly Father, who settest the solitary in families: We commend to thy continual care the homes in which thy people dwell. Put far from them, we beseech thee, every root of bitterness, the desire of vainglory, and the pride of life. Fill them with faith, virtue, knowledge, temperance, patience, godliness. Knit together in constant affection those who, in holy wedlock, have been made one flesh. Turn the hearts of the parents to the children, and the hearts of the children to the parents; and so enkindle fervent charity among us all, that we may evermore be kindly affectioned one to another; through Jesus Christ our Lord. *Amen.*

For Those Who Live Alone (829)

Almighty God, whose Son had nowhere to lay his head: Grant that those who live alone may not be lonely in their solitude, but that, following in his steps, they may find fulfillment in loving you and their neighbors; through Jesus Christ our Lord. *Amen.*

For a Birthday (830)

O God, our times are in your hand: Look with favor, we pray, on your servant *N.* as *he* begins another year. Grant that *he* may grow in wisdom and grace, and strengthen *his* trust in your goodness all the days of *his* life; through Jesus Christ our Lord. *Amen.*

For Travelers (831)

O God, our heavenly Father, whose glory fills the whole creation, and whose presence we find wherever we go: Preserve those who travel [in particular _____]; surround them with your loving care; protect them from every danger; and bring them in safety to their journey's end; through Jesus Christ our Lord. *Amen.*

A Prayer attributed to St. Francis (833)

Lord, make us instruments of your peace. Where there is hatred, let us sow love; where there is injury, pardon; where there is discord, union; where there is doubt, faith; where there is despair, hope; where there is darkness, light; where there is sadness, joy. Grant that we may not so much seek to be consoled as to console; to be understood as to understand; to be loved as to love. For it is in giving that we receive; it is in pardoning that we are pardoned; and it is in dying that we are born to eternal life. *Amen.*

After Receiving Communion (834)

O Lord Jesus Christ, who in a wonderful Sacrament hast left unto us a memorial of thy passion: Grant us, we beseech thee, so to venerate the sacred mysteries of thy Body and Blood, that we may ever perceive within ourselves the fruit of thy redemption; who livest and reignest with the Father and the Holy Spirit, one God, for ever and ever. *Amen.*

Blessings at Meals (835)

Give us grateful hearts, our Father, for all thy mercies, and make us mindful of the needs of others; through Jesus Christ our Lord. *Amen.*

or this

Bless, O Lord, thy gifts to our use and us to thy service; for Christ's sake. *Amen.*

or this

Blessed are you, O Lord God, King of the Universe, for you give us food to sustain our lives and make our hearts glad; through Jesus Christ our Lord. *Amen.*

or this

For these and all his mercies, God's holy Name be blessed and praised; through Jesus Christ our Lord. *Amen.*

Thanksgiving for Heroic Service (839)

O Judge of the nations, we remember before you with grateful hearts the men and women of our country who in the day of decision ventured much for the liberties we now enjoy. Grant that we may not rest until all the people of this land share the benefits of true freedom and gladly accept its disciplines. This we ask in the Name of Jesus Christ our Lord. *Amen.*

Thanksgiving for the Diversity of Races and Cultures (840)

O God, who created all peoples in your image, we thank you for the wonderful diversity of races and cultures in this world. Enrich our lives by ever-widening circles of fellowship, and show us your presence in those who differ most from us, until our knowledge of your love is made perfect in our love for all your children; through Jesus Christ our Lord. *Amen.*